CONTENTS

1 All in the Mind   1

One moment   1

Your 3G mindset   14

So, you want a job?   18

What recruitment consultants want   27

The day of the interview   32

Interview questions and the interviewers who love them   39

2 Classic Interview Questions: the 'Fateful 15'   45

1. Tell me about yourself   46

2. Why are you applying?   52

3. What are your greatest strengths?   54

4. What are your greatest weaknesses?   56

5. What will your skills and ideas bring to this company?   61

6. What's your preferred management style?   62

7. Where do you see yourself in five years' time?   64

8. How would you approach this job?   67

9. What have you achieved elsewhere?   68

10. What did you like and dislike about your last job?   70

11. Tell me about a time you worked in a team   72

12. What do your co-workers say about you?   74

13. How do you deal with stress and failure?   76

14. How much money do you want? 77

15. Show me your creativity 78

3 Career Goal Questions **80**

16. Please describe the job you've applied for 82

17. How did you hear about the position? 83

18. Why do you want to work at this company? 84

19. What motivates you? 85

20. Would you stay with your current employer if they offered you a pay rise? 87

21. Would you be OK with the commute to this job? 89

22. How does this job fit in with your career plan? 90

23. Give me the names of three companies you would like to work for 92

24. Where else have you applied? / Who else are you interviewing with? 94

25. Why have you changed jobs so frequently? 96

26. What is your dream job? 98

27. What's your ideal work environment? 101

28. Why do you want to leave your current job? 102

29. Talk me through (the gaps in) your CV/career history 105

4 Character Questions **109**

30. How was your journey here? 112

31. Where does your boss think you are now? 114

32. What are your core values? 115

33. What are your hobbies and interests? 116

34. Tell me about your first job 117

35. Who do you admire and why? 119

36. If you could bring anyone to this company from where you currently work, who would it be? 121

37. Tell me about a time you dealt with a difficult person 122

38. When were you last angry – and why? 124

WHY YOU?

James Reed is the Chairman of REED, the recruitment specialists. He first joined the company in 1992 after graduating from Harvard Business School; since then REED has more than quadrupled in size and reed.co.uk has become the number one job site in the UK and Europe. REED now receives more than 50 million job applications a year and has delivered over 100 programmes helping more than 140,000 long-term unemployed people back into work. James is co-author of *Put Your Mindset to Work*, winner of the Commuter's Read Prize at the CMI Management Book Awards 2012. He is also a Fellow of the Chartered Institute of Personnel and Development (CIPD).

80003421656

Praise for *Why You?*:

'Takes much of the fear out of preparing for a job interview' *Sunday Post*

'Amazon UK's fastest-selling new read on interview techniques' *City A.M.*

From Amazon:

***** 'Got the job!'

***** 'A must for all interviewees'

***** 'Worth a permanent place on your bookshelf'

***** 'Perfect preparation for any interview'

***** 'Good for employers too!'

***** 'I read this from cover to cover before an interview for a very much wanted job. I did all the exercises it recommend and . . . I got the job!'

***** 'If you are seriously after a job this is essential reading'

***** 'Helped me get my current job!'

***** 'Really useful, gives clear examples and well explained – I got the job so must have been a good buy!'

***** 'Helped me prepare perfectly for interview, giving me real questions that come up – along with excellent tips for how to answer them. Wouldn't have got the job without this book'

WHY YOU?

101 Interview Questions
You'll Never Fear Again

JAMES REED

PORTFOLIO
PENGUIN

PORTFOLIO PENGUIN

UK | USA | Canada | Ireland | Australia
India | New Zealand | South Africa

Portfolio Penguin is part of the Penguin Random House group of companies
whose addresses can be found at global.penguinrandomhouse.com.

First published 2014
Reissued with a new bonus chapter in this edition 2017
001

Copyright © James Reed, 2014, 2017

The moral right of the author has been asserted

Set in 10.75/13.75 pt Berkeley Oldstyle Book
Typeset by Jouve (UK), Milton Keynes
Printed in Great Britain by Clays Ltd, St Ives plc

A CIP catalogue record for this book is available from the British Library

ISBN: 978–0–241–29713–1

Northamptonshire
Libraries & Information
Services
NW

Askews & Holts	

FS
www.fsc.org

For the moment

CONTENTS

39. Tell me about something funny that has happened to you at work   125

40. What is it about this job that you would least look forward to?   127

41. Tell me something about yourself that isn't on your CV   128

42. What do you most dislike about yourself?   131

43. How would you react if I told you that you are not the strongest candidate we have interviewed so far?   133

44. Is it acceptable to lie in business?   134

45. If you could go back and change one thing about your career to date, what would it be?   137

46. What do people assume about you that would be wrong?   139

47. Can you tell me about a time when you stood up for the right thing to do?   140

48. Have you ever stolen a pen from work?   142

49. Did you enjoy school/university?   143

50. Do you know anyone at this company?   145

51. How do you maintain a good work/life balance?   146

52. Are your grades a good indicator of success in this business?   147

53. Would you rather be liked or feared?   149

54. What are your thoughts on the interview process so far?   150

55. Why should I choose you over other candidates?   151

56. Is it OK to spend time at work on non-work stuff, like Facebook or YouTube?   154

57. What are three positive things your boss/colleagues would say about you?   156

58. What has been the biggest setback in your career?   158

59. Your boss overslept and is now late for a client meeting. He calls and asks you to tell the client that he is stuck in traffic – in other words to lie for him. What do you do?   160

CONTENTS

5 Competency Questions — **162**

60. What was the last big decision you had to make? — 163

61. Tell me about a time you've worked to/missed a deadline — 165

62. Tell me about a big change you've had to deal with — 168

63. Tell me about a time you've had to persuade someone to do something — 170

64. Give me an example of something you've tried in your job that hasn't worked. How did you learn from it? — 172

65. Tell me about a time you've disagreed with a senior member of staff — 173

66. If offered the job, what would be your first priority or thing you would change? — 175

67. Why are you a good fit for the company? — 177

68. What was the last thing you taught? — 179

69. How have you ensured maximum value for money when managing resources? — 180

70. Name some top opinion influencers in this industry — 181

71. Most people are good at managing up or down, but usually not both. Which one are you? — 183

72. Which websites do you use personally? Why? — 185

73. How does your personal social media presence affect your employer? — 186

74. How have you improved in the last year? — 188

75. Tell me about a time a client was especially unhappy and what you did to resolve the situation — 190

76. Tell me about a time you made an important decision in the absence of a manager. Why did you reach that decision? — 191

77. Can you tell me about a recent situation where you took the initiative and made something happen? — 193

78. What is the biggest issue between you and your current/previous manager? — 194

79. What is your favourite product/service in the industry? — 195

80. What is 10 per cent of 100? — 198

CONTENTS

81. Tell me about a time you supported a member of your team who was struggling   200

82. In your current job, how many hours a week must you work to get it all done?   201

83. Give an example of a time you've had to improvise to achieve your goal   203

6   Curveball and Creativity Questions   205

84. If you were an animal what would you be?   208

85. Every CV has at least one lie in it. What's yours?   209

86. Have you ever been fired?   210

87. Tell me about a time you went against company policy   214

88. Tell me about your family   216

89. Are you married? Planning to have kids? When did you start your career? Where are you from originally? Do you celebrate any specific religious holidays?   217

90. Where did you last go on holiday?   219

91. Tell me about the last good idea you had   221

92. Would you mind if I approached your former/current employer for a reference?   222

93. What would you guess is the most searched-for phrase on YouTube?   223

94. What books and newspapers do you read?   226

95. Aren't you overqualified for this job?   227

96. Sell me this pen   229

97. Give your CV a mark out of ten   230

98. Our product has seriously antisocial side effects. How do you feel about that?   232

99. How many traffic lights are there in London?   233

100. What haven't I asked you that I should have?   235

101. When can you start?   237

7 Parting Shots   **239**

When it's your turn   239

Last impressions – how to wrap up the interview   255

How to follow up without being a stalker   259

The real answer   263

Bonus Chapter: Ten Extra Tech Questions   **265**

102. How do you keep up with new technology in this industry?   267

103. What will tech do for us in the future?   269

104. Tell me about the biggest technical challenge you've come up against   270

105. Tell me about a time you worked on a project involving a technology that was new to you. How did you approach it?   272

106. What's your favourite piece of software that you use to help you do your job and why?   274

107. How do you manage remote working relationships?   276

108. How would you improve our website/app?   277

109. If you were a tech brand, which one would you be and why?   279

110. If you could create an app that could do anything to improve your life, what would it be?   281

111. How would you explain a database to an eight-year-old in three sentences?   282

Acknowledgements   **285**

ONE

ALL IN THE MIND

'Well, life all comes down to a
few moments. This is one of them'

Wall Street, 1987, 20th Century Fox

One moment

Can the path of a person's entire life come down to what they do in just one or two decisive moments? The guitarist Andy Summers certainly thinks so.

You might not recognize Summers' name but you'll know his work. Summers was one-third of The Police, one of the most successful rock bands of all time.

Maybe you're not a fan, but you would have to agree that Summers, in being a guitarist in a rock band, landed a job that many of us would love to have. His job took him to almost every country in the world. He did creative things all day. He met interesting people and devoted fans. He was paid a ton of money for doing something he loved, something that came naturally to him. Truly, great work if you can get it. So how *did* he get it?

He got it by boarding a London Tube train and sitting down at random next to a drummer named Stewart Copeland. People don't usually talk on the Tube, but for some reason those two struck up a conversation that day. It was a conversation in which they told each other what kind of music they wanted to make. Each convinced the other that he was sincere and suitable. They clicked. They formed a band. They met Sting. They went to work.

Take out that last bit about Sting and you've got a perfect description of what happens at a good job interview: two people talking from the heart about a common interest, each setting out what they have to offer. (Admittedly, this is different from the ritualized job interview that many of us are familiar with.)

When the time came for Summers to write his autobiography, he called it *One Train Later*, because if he'd taken the next train along he wouldn't have met Copeland and none of his enchanted career would have happened. Clearly, it was one of those moments when the entire course of his life could have gone one way or another – just as occurs in a job interview.

Maybe you feel that Summers didn't interview for his job, that he succeeded by having a skill (in his case, playing the guitar) and by honing that skill with hours of practice every day. You'd be right, but skills are never the full picture.

It's more accurate to say Summers was *fully prepared when his moment of destiny presented itself*. He was at a point in his life where he knew what he was good at, and could communicate it to a total stranger in a way that made him seem like the sort of person you would want around.

This is a book about how you can learn to do exactly the same thing.

Knowing your moment

All the evidence is that these moments of life-changing destiny are most likely to present themselves in the form of a job interview.

How you perform in that thirty-to-ninety-minute window will determine what you do for a living, which in turn will shape much of your time on Earth, including:

- **What you do all day:** Approximately one-third of your adult life is spent at work. If you don't enjoy your work, that's one-third of your existence hammered, with no refunds and no re-runs. (To put this into even sharper relief, half the remaining two-thirds of your adult life is spent asleep, or maybe lying awake at night thinking about work.)
- **Where you live and what you see all day:** Where we spend our limited time on this planet is determined largely by where we work, with 90 per cent of us living within an hour of our job. Your job interview is going to determine what you see out of the window all day, be it city skyline or sunrise over the Pacific at 35,000ft.
- **Your income:** When a really good PA can earn more than a junior pilot, who cares about sunrises?
- **Your life partner:** If you go to nightclubs hoping to find that special someone, statistically you'll have more luck working behind the bar than on the dance floor. Nineteen per cent of us meet our spouses at work – it's the most common place for love to start, by far. And should you get lucky with a colleague, you can rejoice in the fact that divorce rates are lower than average among couples who meet at work, probably because they have a common interest.

- **When you'll die:** There's a good reason your life-assurance company asks what you do for a living. It's a proven fact that, whether you're a personal trainer or someone who sits down in an office all day, your health is subject to the physical impact of your job.
- **Your social status:** You are what you do. Of all the professions, it seems doctors and nurses get most of our admiration and trust. (Politicians and bankers, not so much.)
- **Your personal happiness:** Job satisfaction is, of course, hugely important. Interestingly, more than one study has shown that if you want to be happily employed you should pick up some scissors and learn to cut hair. Most hairdressing salon owners are happier in their work than any of their clients.

So that's your time, your money, your love life, your horizon, your health, your social status and your happiness – all determined in part at a job interview. If life really does boil down to a few decisive moments, the interview is surely one of them. Like it or not, people who are good at interviews tend to be good at life.

With so much resting on the outcome, it's no wonder interviewees get nervous. But as scary as it is to meet one's destiny in a job interview, you are at least told about the meeting in advance and given a chance to prepare. You get more notice of your key moment than Andy Summers got for his. Better still, with interviews you only need to practise a *little* harder than the rest, not for hours a day like musicians do.

If you think of interviews that way, they'll suddenly seem less like a trial and more like a lucky big break, a tip-off, an inside advantage, one that you should seize with everything you have.

What have you done for destiny lately?

Learning how to get just a *little* better at job interviews is one of the best-value things you can do for yourself, pound for pound and minute for minute.

Despite this, most people spend more time preparing their dinner than preparing for an interview. Maybe they're scared, knowing there is so much at risk. Fear often creeps in whenever the stakes are high, closely followed by procrastination, resulting in many candidates feeling the same way about interview preparation as Orson Welles felt about flying: a mixture of 'boredom and terror'.

In truth, almost everybody procrastinates about job interviews – which means less competition for you. Employers rarely complain about having too many great-performing interviewees to choose from. So, for those who would push a little harder than the rest, success at interview is there for the taking.

The best preparation consists of finding heartfelt and useful answers to certain key questions – and there aren't so many questions that they can't all be mastered by the average person in a few evenings' work.

At Reed, we believe that even the most thorny and exotic interview questions are just permutations of a tiny superset of key questions. Get good at these key questions and all the other questions will take care of themselves. If you want to make a start right now, go straight to the 'Classic Interview Questions' section in Chapter 2.

How to use this book

It's important to know that this book will not teach you how to 'game' interviews by using canned answers. You will be offered some broad illustrative responses, but I strongly suggest that you don't parrot those illustrations word for word. Believe me, *canned answers don't work*. I employ approximately 3,000 people and most of them conduct job interviews for a living. I can assure you that they hear canned answers every day, as do the employers who make up Reed's clients – and every single one of those canned answers is played out.

The problem is getting worse all the time, thanks to the internet being one big echo chamber. The phrase 'interview questions' alone is searched half a million times a month on Google, not to mention all the other similar searches, such as 'What to say in interview'.

What happens is that candidates click on the first one or two results, memorize the answers and then feel they've done all the interview prep they need, when in fact they've just made it harder for employers to find out who they really are. It's as though some people think of interviews as a game of catchphrase bingo, rather than a sincere conversation between two strangers.

Pretending to be someone you're not is wrong. It is also much harder work for you in the long run. Nobody ever got fired for turning out to be exactly the person they seemed to be in interview, but plenty of people have been fired for spoofing their way into a post they weren't right for, and, before being fired, they probably suffered for a long time, thrashing away at a job they couldn't actually do.

The other reason to avoid canned responses is that there is surprisingly little consensus among interviewers about what constitutes a good answer. That much became clear when

Reed conducted twenty or so workshops among its recruitment consultants for this book. In those sessions, a bad answer was easily identified but a good one was often a matter of taste and much debate.

But as useless as canned answers are, their example does at least bring us to the heart of this book. Canned answers are bad because they get in the way of letting the employer find out who you are. And *who you really are* is becoming just as important as what you can do. Go back a couple of decades and a job interview would have been almost exclusively about skills and experience; these days your interview is just as likely to be about your personality and your mindset. As has been written a million times elsewhere, the world is changing very rapidly these days, partly because skills and expertise are becoming increasingly commodified and distributed. In this environment, your personality comes to the fore. What that means for job interviews is that a computer programmer's ability to convey their hopes and dreams and quirks now has almost as much bearing on their chances of success as their ability to program. Once again, you might not like such a state of affairs – but it absolutely is how things are now. Firms don't hire CVs, they hire people. They always have, but more so now than ever.

How I wrote this book

I've always believed in the idea that a team is a genius. Consequently, it was clear to me that the interview wisdom found in this book should be crowdsourced. And since I'm proud to be the Chairman of the Reed Group, the recruitment agency started in 1960 by my father Sir Alec Reed and now the UK's single largest aggregator of jobs and job interviews, I was fortunate to have access to the views of a very large crowd indeed. (By the way, what follows is the first and only bit of tub-thumping for Reed you'll see in this book, although, unavoidably, it can't be the last mention.)

On any given day Reed's website features 250,000 jobs from 12,000 employers; we receive more than 180 million visits a year and have over 11 million CVs on our database. More importantly, we employ 2,000 recruitment consultants. These consultants spend their entire working day matching jobs to candidates. In most cases they meet the firm offering the job and they also meet or speak with the candidates looking to win that job. This gives consultants a unique insight into what works, both from the employers' point of view and from that of the successful and unsuccessful candidates. Consultants will often ring both parties after the interview to find out what was asked and which answers went down well. Just as usefully, they hear about which answers bring interviews to an early and uncomfortable end on a daily basis.

There are literally hundreds of questions you might be asked at interview, but you shouldn't care about the full set. You only want to know which questions you're most likely to be asked – and who can blame you? You can't prepare for all of them.

With so much traffic to Reed's website, it's very easy for us to survey a large number of employers about the questions they're most likely to ask – and that's exactly what we did for this book.

What follows, then, is the most rigorously data-tested survey of the interview questions that you're most likely to be asked this year. If that doesn't justify the price of the book alone, write to me at James@jamesreed.com and tell me what would. I'll put it into the next edition. Equally, let me know if you found this book useful during an interview, and what questions you were asked; you can Tweet me using #WhyYou.

But Reed didn't just gather questions. I also hit the road to talk to our consultants about what constitutes a good and a bad answer for each. These workshops were among the most fun I've ever had at Reed and the wisdom that emerged from them is here on every page. Take it from me: recruitment consultants know interview questions better than anyone.

Throughout this book, you'll see that each of our 101 questions are headed with two short sections of text – 'The Real Question' and a 'Top-line Tactic'. These are for your insight and convenience, respectively. The Real Question is essentially the interviewer's inner dialogue, telling you what he or she is really thinking but is (hopefully) too nice to say. The Top-line Tactic is simply a summary of our recommendation for answering that particular question, expressed in a single sentence. The former is there to help you understand, the latter is there to help you remember what you might say.

The digested read

If you only take away four points from this book, make them these:

- The best person you can be at interview is yourself.
- The way you talk about who you are and what you can become counts for more than a good CV or an expensive education.
- Every interview question that you can be asked is a variation of a handful of underlying fundamental questions.
- To an employer, a job is a problem to be solved. All other concerns are secondary, including yours.

Let's look at those in turn.

The best person you can be at interview is yourself

This might not sound like new advice and it is often reported as clichéd. It's not clichéd – it's vital.

Interviewers are only human. They want to feel an emotional connection with a real person, not a politician. They love it when that connection happens in an interview room, but it happens less often than it might, because an interview room is an artificial environment, one that can easily prompt artificial behaviour, stilted conversation and awkward pauses. It's usually not where you see people at their best, even though that's what everyone in the room wants to see.

After wading through countless canned answers, awkward pauses and half-truths, interviewers are often left craving a genuine encounter with a sincere human being. If you speak from the heart and don't exaggerate, bluff or waffle, you'll be giving interviewers what they crave. They'll remember you for it, even if you're not right for the job.

....

Many interviewers will keep a rejected candidate on file in case something suitable comes up; many candidates have successfully landed a job this way.

....

Oddly, being yourself in an interview situation is always harder than it sounds. It's risky too, certainly in terms of getting a job. It's not risky in terms of getting the right job.

It's not about your CV: it's about who you are and what you can become

Most people start their interview prep by dusting off their CV and thinking of a few things to say about the sentences on that fabled sheet of A4. But if you've been invited for interview, your CV will suddenly be far less important than it has always seemed to you, because by interview stage, an interviewer has already got most of what they need from your CV. They're now in interview mode, not CV mode. In interview mode, the primary assessment is of you and your personality, less so your work history. Also, your CV is all about the past, about a world of skills and technology and institutions that are either gone already or perhaps soon will be. The future arrives relentlessly.

All that any business can do about the future is to employ people who can cope with change. If you can lead change – relish it, even – you *will* be in demand. Employers want people who will thrive in a workplace that might be unrecognizable three years from now.

That's why anyone who bases their interview technique entirely around the contents of their CV is looking in the wrong direction. The interviewer will be looking forward, into a future they can barely make out. No one knows what's going to happen next. The CEO doesn't know. You don't know. Your interviewer doesn't know either. You can expect job interviews to reflect that uncertainty – and to select on the basis of it too.

The good news for you is that future-proofing yourself is a learnable skill that you can demonstrate in interview. It's all a matter of adopting the right mindset (there's more on mindset in the next section).

There are only fifteen interview questions that count

No matter what you read elsewhere, Reed believes there are only fifteen questions that an interviewer might ask you.

Sure, there are hundreds of interview questions you might be asked, but *every interview question out there is just a variation on one of fifteen themes.*

We know because we've counted. When reed.co.uk surveyed thousands of employers and asked which question they're most likely to ask in an interview, the same few themes kept emerging. Many interview questions are just different ways of asking the same thing. Out of the hundreds of questions we received, we found that just fifteen were truly unique. We've called them the 'Fateful 15', for reasons Andy Summers would understand – each one has the potential to change the direction of your life for better or worse, for ever.

This book is going to help you discover honest, personal and impressive answers to all fifteen. Once you've got that knack, you'll see how those fifteen questions fit into every aspect of working life. So equipped, you'll be more productive and employable regardless of what happens in any one interview.

Each one of the fifteen has a 'question behind the question' – an emotional theme that extends beyond the surface words. It is this deeper emotional theme that you must listen for, and to which you must address your answer.

If you can come up with scintillating answers for these fifteen questions – and learn to identify each one in the heat of the moment – then you will be good at interviews. And as we've seen, being good at interviews means being good at life, work and almost everything else. That thought might seem painful and unfair to some, but it's always been true.

But before we start that, we need to be clear about why job vacancies appear in the first place. It's not because someone wants you to have a job. It's because someone, somewhere, has a problem.

To an employer, a job is a problem to be solved

Jobs exist in two completely different universes at the same time.

In one universe – let's call it the 'personal universe', the one that we experience as interviewees and as people – jobs make life worth living.

In the personal universe, jobs provide us with a home, friends, stimulation, conversation, holidays, a new car and so on. This is the world of work that we recognize and that so many of us crave. Each year the global market-research firm Gallup carries out a survey asking thousands of adults in over two hundred countries a very simple question: **'What do you want most?'** The most common answer, every year and all over the world, is, **'A good job.'** There's something in us that wants to work. Consequently, no one can be blamed for wanting a job and all the life-affirming things that come from it.

But jobs inhabit a second universe too – let's call it the entrepreneur's universe – and in this universe **a job does not exist to keep you happy**.

In this universe, jobs are a by-product of an entrepreneur's desire to build their own business, a business the entrepreneur hopes will solve all of his or her problems via solving other people's problems. For entrepreneurs, their business is often all that stands between them and financial ruin, so they fight hard to keep it going. It's worth remembering that every company, be it Marks and Spencer or your local corner shop, is either run by one of these scrappy individuals or was started by one. Companies differ in the extent to which they retain their founders' 'survive-or-die' ethic, but it's echoing off the walls in most companies, certainly in the companies that have progressed and survived.

In this universe, your interviewer is best thought of as someone with a stack of problems which they will pay to solve. Collectively, these problems are known as your job and, to be blunt, that's all any job ever was. It's a rather stark and unemotional way of looking at life, but it's no less true for that.

Too bad, then, that many candidates can glimpse jobs in one universe only. They see a job as a means of achieving their personal economic or psychological advancement, and forget that a job is primarily about solving problems on behalf of someone else. This personal bias surfaces in their answers.

It might be going too far to suggest that you should think of your interviewer as a motorist who's broken down by the side of the road and in need of help, but it's not a bad starting point. It's certainly better than thinking of the interviewer as a food truck by the side of the road, as so many candidates do.

A bad interviewee, then, defines a job as something that will solve all their problems. Good interviewees know that a 'job' is what happens when you can solve someone else's problem – so start pitching your answers that way.

Your 3G mindset

The truth is that interviewing – and impressing employers in general – is much less about hard skills than you've probably been led to believe and much more about how you think. In this book we'll spend whole sections covering questions of motivation and personality as well as softer competencies like decision making, leadership, adaptability and trustworthiness. And what's another word for all these factors, the sum of your approach to your job and your life, the fundamental lens that colours how you view and respond to your work? Your *mindset*.

Talking about your mindset is central to this book because it is also central to my approach to recruitment. In 2011 I co-authored a book with Dr Paul G. Stoltz, a leading expert on human resilience. We conducted in-depth research into the preferences of employers globally, asking them to tell us what sets candidates apart in today's fast-changing, ultra-competitive job market. What we found is covered in depth in our book, *Put Your Mindset to Work*, but let's now recap a few key points from it.

How much does mindset matter?

It's no surprise that employers would prefer a trustworthy person who shows accountability, but the employers that Paul and I canvassed for their views went much, much further when they spoke about how much a person's mindset accounts for hiring, retention and promotion. When asked if they would choose someone with the right mindset who lacks all the skills desired for a position or someone who has all the skills but not the ideal mindset, an astonishing **96 per cent of employers said they'd pick mindset over skills**. That bears repeating: 96 per cent value mindset over skills.

But how much difference does mindset make? On average, employers said they would trade seven normal workers with a so-so outlook for just one with a great mindset. Having the right approach to your work makes you seven times more valuable to an employer.

In-depth interviews with executives backed up these numbers. Top company boss after top company boss came to the same conclusion as John Suranyi, former president of DIRECTV: 'Mindset is everything.'

Caitlin Dooley, a recruiter for Facebook, agreed that workers at the social networking company 'absolutely have to have the right mindset, period. That's what's driving us into the future.'

If you can wrap your head around just how valuable employers find mindset then you won't be surprised by some of the other findings from the book. Employers repeatedly said that while the right mindset helps you gain and grow the right skills, the reverse is not true. Great skills do not lead you to a better mindset. No wonder, then, that when times turn tough, those with the best mindset are much less liable to be let go, while in better times, they're far more likely to be promoted. The right mindset is also correlated with higher earning potential – those with the right outlook generally out-earn those who lack it.

And how about hiring, the subject of this book? What data is there on the impact of having the right mindset on your ability to land the job of your dreams? It's unequivocal: get your mindset right and convey that to your potential employer and you are three times more likely to get and keep the job that you want.

What mindset are employers looking for?

Now that you know the right mindset can triple your chances of finding a great job, you'll be keen to know what constitutes the mindset that's most desired by employers.

The most desired traits neatly fall into three simple categories, which together can be encompassed with the easy-to-remember term '3G Mindset'. The three Gs in question are *Global*, *Good* and *Grit*.

- **Global** is your vantage point. It's about how far you see, reach and go to understand and address everyday challenges and issues. It's about thinking big, making connections and being open. *Key qualities*: adaptability, flexibility, relationship building, collaborative focus, openness, innovativeness.
- **Good** is your bedrock. Whether you approach the world in way that truly benefits those around you determines how positive or negative your contribution will be. Those who aren't good can have an impact, but it's rarely for the

betterment of others or the organization. *Key qualities*: honesty, trustworthiness, loyalty, sincerity, fairness and kindness.

- **Grit** is your fuel cell. This is the tenacity and resilience that drives your accomplishment despite adversity and setbacks. *Key qualities*: commitment, accountability, determination, drive, energy.

Do these three concepts blend into each other? Of course, but that only makes them more dynamic, as each of the Gs reinforces and powers the others. Only all three working in tandem makes for a truly exceptional – and highly desirable – person. Consider which of the key qualities are present in you and try to make it clear from your answers that you possess them.

How does that affect me?

It's crystal clear that having the right mindset can give you the edge when it comes to securing your next job and can even help you overcome any skills gaps you might have on your CV. Keep that in mind as you go through this book and start selecting and practising your own answers to likely interview questions.

You may be asked to talk about a time you missed a deadline, or even to figure out something wacky like how many golf balls fit in a Boeing 747, but underneath all the things you might be asked in the interview room, no matter how different they seem on the surface, runs a constant, unspoken question every hiring manager is dying to get the answer to: *Do you have the right mindset to make a truly exceptional contribution here?*

Those golf-ball questions are just a proxy to determine whether your thinking is global, i.e. open, innovative and wide ranging. That deadline question is there to test your grit – when the going got tough, how did you respond?

Keep this fundamental truth in mind as you go through this book and prepare for your interview. Try to weave some small proof of each of the 3Gs into each answer you give, while also of course addressing whatever is asked. Bit by bit, you'll paint a picture for the interviewer of a candidate with that golden ticket to excellence – the 3G mindset. Manage that trick and you'll triple your chances of landing a great job. Research proves it.

So, you want a job?

If you're reading this book, you're either thinking of changing jobs or entering/re-entering the workforce. You'll find all the tools you need to do that within these pages, but before you get started with the nitty-gritty of preparing for interviews, there is very important preliminary work to be done.

'No worries,' you might be thinking, 'I've got several job listings printed out and a comprehensive list of my skills right here.'

Those things will be incredibly useful a bit further along in the process. They're not the right place to start, however. Beginning your job search by combing online job boards or working up a skills inventory is like jumping into the rapids and then trying to inflate your raft while staying afloat; you're diving into an emotionally draining process without a sturdy understanding of your motivations and goals for changing jobs. You need to know where you're going, why, and how you plan to get there, before you start assembling your toolkit for the adventure. Not only must you be right for the job, the job must also be right for you.

This may sound like an optional extra, but be warned that job seekers who fail to reflect on why they're unhappy with their current job and what they need to be more satisfied in their next one often end up jumping out of the frying pan and into the fire. Without adequate reflection, you could easily end up spending weeks or months on a difficult search only to end up in a role that suits you even less than the one you left.

Examine your motives

To make sure your efforts pay off in the form of a step up in your career, you must answer a deceptively simple question: *Why do you want this job?*

On the surface this sounds like the kind of question you should be able to answer in a second, and in some instances, for example when you love your present role and career trajectory but simply hate your toxic boss, it is.

But many job changers simply act from a vague feeling of dissatisfaction, boredom or a nagging sense that there must be something better out there. If that's you then take some time to dig deeper. Ask yourself: Do I really need to change jobs? Looking for work is exhausting and difficult. Sometimes you're far better off simply putting some of that effort into improving conditions at your current job. If you feel stuck, for instance, could a conversation with your boss about developing a plan for career advancement be a better first step than contacting a recruiter? No job is perfect, and if your impulse is to jump ship the second things get difficult, rest assured, progress in your career will be limited. Make sure you're leaving for a good reason. If discussions with your boss prove fruitless, *then* you have a good reason.

What counts as a good reason? As mentioned above, a

truly toxic work environment is a great reason. Flee immediately and don't look back if you're the victim of bullying, harassment or verbal haranguing by supervisors. If objective data shows you're underpaid, and your efforts to get what you're worth go nowhere, you're fully justified in starting a search. Maybe your life circumstances have changed and your current job no longer fits your needs, or you've been working in a particular industry or role long enough to know it's truly a bad fit for your skills or personality. Good reasons to leave are plentiful. Just make sure you have one.

Choose a target

Don't simply run away from your old job looking for whatever random opportunity happens to come along. You need to think not only about your motivations for leaving, but also your desired destination. Once you've determined why your old employer is a bad fit, you can consider what sort of job would be free from those drawbacks. This can be simple if you're making a relatively small move within a familiar industry in order to improve your pay, working conditions or prospects for advancement. However, if you're looking to make more radical changes, you'll need to think more carefully. Questions to ponder include:

- What part of my job energizes me? What drains me?
- Am I creative, independent, a lover of routine? Will my personality align with this new job?
- What are my strengths and weaknesses? Are they suitable for the role?
- What sort of work environment do I enjoy? Do I like sitting in front of a computer? Do I like to be among people? On my feet? Outdoors?

- What sort of income do I need?
- What is the outlook for the sector I am considering? Is it growing? Are many jobs likely to be available in the future?

If you're considering making a big leap in your career, there are plenty of tools to help you assess whether the job you're considering will be a good match for you personally. A host of both free and paid assessors such as MAPP, Myers Briggs and Career Key are available to help pair job seekers with appropriate careers. Such an assessment is unlikely to provide a silver bullet, landing you the perfect job simply by filling out a multiple choice quiz, but if you're truly struggling to settle on a career direction, they may provide some food for thought.

In cases where you're taking a real leap into the unknown, dipping a toe into the water before you make a radical change, either by interning, engaging in a short job placement or a job-shadowing scheme, or speaking with others already working in the sector, can also be valuable. Remember that you will spend something like eight hours a day at your new job. You don't want to choose it without careful self-examination and a really honest look at your abilities and preferences. Don't rush this step. If you get it wrong you're still going to end up unhappy, even if you do everything else in this book perfectly.

Getting there

You've pondered, considered, researched and reflected, and now you've settled on just the sort of job you're after. Congratulations! This is more than many unhappy workers do and should stand you in good stead for the rest of your job search (and make it easy to nail any 'motivation' questions that come up in your interviews). What's the next step?

You've done the hard work to figure out why you want your target job, now it's time to figure out why they should want you. We've already spoken about the primacy of having the right mindset, but skills still count for something too – and so you need to do a skills audit. Doing this well is a two-part process. The first step is to list all the things you have to offer an employer. Then, you'll want to look at what employers are looking for from you.

To get started, draw three columns labelled 'Knowledge-based skills', 'Transferable skills' and 'Personal traits'. In the first column list all the nuts-and-bolts things you've learned to do at work, whether that is develop online marketing plans, operate a fork-lift or drafting engaging lesson plans. Don't limit yourself to your last couple of jobs. Draw on your entire life experience. You can whittle these down later, but for now just do a brain dump and get everything out on paper at the start.

In column two list all the less tangible but still valuable skills you bring to an employer. These are things like your organizational abilities, public speaking experience or attention to detail. Don't be shy – now is not the time for modesty. Finally, list things that are intrinsic to your personality that employers would find valuable, such as your strong sense of ethics or innate creativity.

These columns contain the raw materials for your skills audit, but think of it as a pile of timber, nails and random building supplies. It's valuable but formless. To make something useful of these skills, you'll need to assemble them in such a way that you manage to create the ideal profile for your target job. You'll need the equivalent of a blueprint – a clear idea of what the companies you want to work for are looking for. Luckily, there's no mystery here. They regularly make that information public in the form of job ads. Trawl through descriptions of the jobs you'd like to have and pull out all the key skills and abilities these employers are after.

You can supplement this research with other sources. Trade publications or industry networking events are great places to learn what skills are valued in your niche. Online tools like O*NET offer lists of key competencies for many jobs.

You now know what skills you have and what skills the employers you're targeting are looking for. Hopefully, most of these line up (you might want to consider further training or other professional development if they don't).

Where your skills match those desired, take a moment to critically rate your abilities. It's important not only to know which skills you possess, but also what level of skill you've attained. Your messy initial list should now be narrowed down to a handful of key skills that your target employers value highly and which you have in abundance. What's next?

Prove it

You can say you are an absolute rock star when it comes to skills A, B and C, but employers aren't going to believe you without evidence. So take a look at your narrowed-down list of skills and start picking through your past work accomplishments for stories that prove you can really do what you say you can. The best evidence in many areas of business is quantifiable, so if you want to persuade a hiring manager that you indeed 'excel at opening up new sales territories' you need to come up with not only an example of a time you did just that, but also the percentage increase in revenue that resulted from those efforts.

Increased sales or cost savings make for great evidence, but there are other sorts of proof you can offer as well. Have you won any prizes or awards? Completed any qualifications or training? Have customers provided any positive feedback you could cite? Can you provide a portfolio of examples, photos, clippings, models, etc.? Whatever form of evidence you select, you'll need to build a solid case for each of the key skills you want to highlight.

Putting it all together

At this stage you've developed a rock solid product – yourself – and gathered all the information about its benefits and features you'll need in order to sell it to potential employers. The final stage is marketing it. Put yourself in the shoes of the hiring manager who placed the job ad. If you've ever been involved in hiring, you will know such ads usually result in a biblical flood of applications. The job market is never a breeze, even during the best of times, and almost every job posting leads to the company being inundated with CVs of all quality levels. That's an immense amount of information to sort through.

No wonder, then, that various studies show hiring managers spend only a few seconds reviewing each CV. Think of these time-pressed managers as akin to supermarket shoppers surveying the toothpaste shelves or the pasta sauce aisle. With hundreds of contenders all screaming for their attention, they have no choice but to lean on branding. Which product catches my eye? Which is most attractively packaged?

Like a breakfast cereal or new formula of cleaning product, your application needs to stand out quickly in a high-information environment. That means the most essential work still remains to be done – you need to condense the skills and evidence you rounded up into a concise, compelling pitch. The experts refer to the final product of this exercise in various ways, but whether it's your 'elevator pitch' delivered at a networking event, a 'statement of personal brand' used as a yardstick to guide all your communications, or written down as the 'summary' atop your CV, your pitch needs to serve the same purpose: it must quickly communicate what you can offer an employer and compel them to want to find out more.

What makes for a good pitch? First, it should be short. If you write it down it should take up no more than a few lines. If you speak it aloud, consider thirty seconds your maximum (the term 'elevator pitch' was coined because you should be able to deliver it in the lift before it reaches your floor). Second, it should be free of jargon and crystal clear in its meaning. If a word seems overused, superficial or clichéd to you, a hiring manager will likely agree. Phrases like 'results-oriented' and 'hard-working' will not help you stand out. Finally, and most importantly, your pitch must highlight not just your skills but also the impressive results that stemmed from them.

Is that a lot to ask of a simple blurb? Absolutely. That's why it's essential you write it down, edit it carefully and solicit feedback from professionals you trust. When you're done, the result might look something like one of these:

Bilingual international sales professional with 10+ years' experience leading efforts to grow new, global markets. Proven track record of developing and retaining large accounts. Strengths include building client relationships and cross-cultural communication. MBA degree.

Experienced leader of substance addiction counsellors with an in-depth knowledge of both the psychological and sociological issues associated with substance abuse. Expertise in both individual and group counselling. Lowered readmission by 25 per cent over four years.

Do these pitches contain all the information their writers rounded up when auditing their skills? Of course not; they're distillations of that fact-finding. But the work won't go to waste. It means that an interviewer's request for more information on, say, the first candidate's 'proven track record building new markets' can easily be met with an example, numbers to back it up and the detail to make it convincing. Is there more to say about the second candidate's impressive 25 per cent reduction in readmissions? Certainly. Now the interviewer will be sure to ask for details, giving the candidate an opportunity to shine.

The final ingredients

As this pitch will not only guide your written communication but also your in-person interviewing, it's also important to practise delivering it aloud. You could craft the finest pitch ever committed to paper and it would be worth precisely nothing if you bumbled your delivery, acted sheepish and inserted 'uhs' and 'ums' between every other word. Confidence is the final secret ingredient of a great pitch.

As we discuss later, confidence is largely a matter of being comfortable in your own skin – of knowing yourself. The self-reflection and research about your career goals suggested earlier in this chapter should go a long way towards helping you achieve the required level of self-understanding. But if you're still occasionally bothered by doubts and fears, your best bet is to confront them head on. Take a moment and really listen to the chatter inside your head.

Do you find yourself constantly worrying that your pitch will reveal you as a fraud? Or maybe your concerns are financial, and you need a job quickly so you can meet your next rental or mortgage payment. You might think listening carefully to your inner critic will give it more power, but if you take the time to actually pay attention to your fears, you're in a better position to overcome them.

Try this trick: Turn each 'What if X?' into a 'How am I going to handle X?' and come up with an answer. If you're worried about seeming like a fraud, respond to that fear by deciding what you'll say if your integrity is questioned. Armed with all your evidence and skills, you should have no trouble convincing any doubter that you can do everything you say you can. And yes, while it would be difficult if your job search went on longer than hoped, perhaps a contingency plan such as taking on a bit of consultancy or temporary work to bridge the gap would help calm your nerves.

Whatever technique you employ, confronting fear and overcoming doubt are the essential final ingredients in developing your pitch. You've already gathered the necessary materials by listing your skills, drafted a blueprint to use them by researching the skills required for your dream job, built a sturdy structure by buttressing your pitch with concrete evidence, and made sure the finish sparkled by writing, editing and practising it. Don't be like the homeowner whose property fails to sell because dirty dishes have been left in the sink and smelly shoes in the hallway. True confidence is the final bit of polish and staging you need to make yourself irresistible to hiring managers.

What recruitment consultants want

Not every job goes through a recruiter, of course, but if you are thinking of using one then what follows should greatly improve your chances of a successful outcome.

Although recruitment agencies can be a great resource for

job seekers, using one isn't a guarantee of success. In order for your experience with an agency to be productive and pleasant for both parties, it's important you come armed with a little bit of basic knowledge about how the recruitment industry works and how to get the most out of your agency.

The basics of the business – how do recruitment agencies make their money?

This is a sensible question to ask and has a straightforward answer. Whenever a candidate put forward by the agency is hired by a company working with the recruiter, the agency is paid a finder's fee. Thus it is in the agency's interest to get you hired. While you as the candidate should never be charged for going through a recruiter, how an agency makes its money will affect how a recruiter can and cannot help you.

The best way to think of it is that an agency finds people for jobs – not just jobs for people. The recruiter's role is to find suitable candidates for the jobs he or she is asked to fill by employers. Of course, a good recruiter is likely to have excellent jobs available in a wide variety of fields, and will also actively engage with their clients to search out new and creative career opportunities on your behalf.

What you can expect

Coming into a recruitment agency with the right set of expectations is key to a happy and productive relationship with your consultant.

First, you need to know what you can expect from your recruiter. As with any industry, there are better and worse agencies, and better and worse consultants. A good one will work with you collaboratively to find the right job for you.

That means taking the time to share their expertise about the job market and what employers are looking for now and offering you advice on your personal presentation, CV and interviewing skills to give you the best chance of landing a great job. Again, you should never be asked to pay a fee of any kind for this sort of help.

Job hunting is stressful. It's good to have an ally by your side, so choose your agencies and consultants with care. Someone who doesn't take the time to discuss your needs, preferences and abilities is unlikely to pitch you very well to prospective employers. The same goes for your personal connection. If you find your consultant cold, unpleasant, overbearing or boring, chances are employers will too. Are you happy for this person to represent you? Can you develop a good working relationship with them or do they make you feel uncomfortable and undervalued? Appointing a consultant who both listens to and supports you will help immensely in your career search.

With rights come responsibilities

You have the right to expect professionalism and a friendly attitude from your consultant, but as in many areas of life, this is a two-way street. If you want to get the best from a good consultant, you need to be a good candidate.

When you contact an agency, the first step is usually a meeting to assess your skills and desires. It will help greatly if you come prepared with a well-crafted CV and a good sense of what you actually want out of your job search (see 'So, you want a job?' on p. 18). No consultant can help you find what you're looking for if you don't have the foggiest idea what that is. Treat this initial meeting like an interview – prepare for it well and present yourself in the best light. This will also show the agent that you can be trusted to represent yourself well if you are sent to interviews.

Don't be afraid to ask about the recruitment process and how long things usually take. Busy agents who have been through the process countless times often forget that a candidate does not have the same understanding of the recruitment business's inner workings. If you hear an unfamiliar term, ask what it means.

Part of that two-way street is that, while the consultant will be representing you to prospective employers, you'll also be representing the agency to those who interview you. How you behave reflects directly on the consultant who put you up for the job. Be professional and do your best at every interview your agency arranges. If you do, they'll be happy to send you out again.

Recruitment consultants, like professionals everywhere, are incredibly busy and communication sometimes suffers under the pressure of day-to-day tasks. You will help both them and yourself by keeping in touch after your initial meeting. Check in regularly via phone or email to make sure you remain at the forefront of their mind. Attend any networking events the agency arranges. Get in touch if you spot a job on the agency's website you're interested in. Also, be reachable. The recruitment business is fast paced and time is often of the essence. When your agent calls or emails, they probably need an immediate response. The more promptly you reply, the more likely you are to land a job.

After you attend an interview, your consultant should offer feedback on your performance and advice on how to improve it. Treat feedback positively – it's one of the most valuable tools an agency can offer you. If you were on your own, you'd rarely receive such useful information. Use it to improve your chances next time. If your consultant is slow to provide feedback, it's perfectly acceptable to ask.

Agencies are an incredible resource and can provide a great deal of help and some essential support during the extremely difficult process of job hunting, but they are only one weapon in your armoury. Even if you've found great consultants to work with you should still continue actively to search for a job on your own in order to optimize your chances of success.

Recruiters' pet hates

The foregoing might be described as the 'dos' of dealing with recruiters, but there are also some 'don'ts'. Chief among them is lying. It's pointless to get creative with the truth about your skills and abilities. You will be found out at your first interview, embarrassing yourself and enraging your consultant in the process. Be honest or your agent can't help you.

A slightly less destructive but still annoying behaviour is when a candidate refuses to compromise their unrealistic, sky-high expectations. Someone just out of university isn't going to be made sales director, nor can even the best recruiter in the business parlay a poor CV into an amazing position. Be honest about your abilities, both with your recruiter and yourself, and don't expect an agency to miraculously fix your faults for you.

Remain enthusiastic and reliable. You came in and told the agent how very excited you were to get down to interviewing, and it's terribly frustrating to arrange an interview only for the candidate to go missing or lose interest. Recruiters dislike timewasters as much as anyone else.

If you keep these points in mind, choose both your agency and your consultant with care, and follow the best practices for candidates outlined above, then your recruitment agency can be a rock solid ally in your hunt for an amazing opportunity.

The day of the interview

Lots of interview advice focuses on the nuts and bolts of the day of the interview – when you should arrive, what colour belt to wear, what to eat for breakfast. Not this book. It's not, of course, that basic logistics aren't important. Getting them wrong can cost you the job, so I'll highlight a couple of fundamentals here, but the most important thing about these sorts of issues is simply getting them out of the way.

If the goal of a job interview is to present the best possible version of your true self and make a real human connection with the interviewer, then worrying about whether you chose the right accessories or noted down the second interviewer's name is unlikely to help you much. When it comes to the day of the interview, the most important thing to do is *remove the stressors and mishaps* that can stop you from showcasing what you have to offer the company.

So how can you accomplish that aim? In truth, you probably learned everything you need to excel at interview-day etiquette from your mother. Be punctual, but not too early. (Showing up more than fifteen minutes before the scheduled time makes you annoying rather than prompt.) It's obviously worse to be late, however, so make sure you know where you're going and how long it will take to get there – if you've any doubt, a practice journey to the interview location a few days before the main event could help relieve anxiety. If it looks as though you'll be early, you can always sit for a few minutes in a coffee shop or take a short walk. Giving yourself some time to calm your nerves might actually be a great idea.

Pack your job interview toolkit a day or two beforehand, not hours before. Include copies of your CV, references and the job description, as well as the name and telephone numbers of the people you're meeting on the off chance you run into difficulties en route. Throw some mints into your bag – but make sure you're not sucking one as you're called in. With all that done, you're now free to focus on what really matters on the day of the big interview – confidence and making a good first impression.

What is confidence?

Take a minute and think of some of the people who have impressed you with their confidence. Do they all have the looks of Brad Pitt, the charisma of Steve Jobs, the intellect of Stephen Hawking? Chances are, the answer is no. Every one of us has encountered everyday people without any genius-level talents or incredible natural gifts who seem to radiate an unflappable sense of confidence. What sets those people apart?

It's not that they're all extroverts with a knack for sales and a hearty handshake. Many of the most impressive candidates in the recruitment business are the shyer, quieter types rather than flashy self-promoters. But all the candidates who attract notice for their confidence have one thing in common – they're comfortable in their own skin. They know who they are, what they want, what they're good at and where they're weak.

Confidence, in other words, isn't a matter of bluster, or even of possessing any particular talent. Confidence is a matter of self-awareness and acceptance, of owning who you really are. Knowing that will put control back in your own hands.

Especially, stop worrying that you're not the 'confident type'. Everyone can be the confident type. Thinking of confidence not as a character trait but as clear-eyed understanding of yourself puts you on the road to developing it.

Using this book to prepare your answers to the fifteen fundamental interview questions that you're likely to be asked will make you think deeply about your strengths, weaknesses, skills and goals – and how they match with the job you are pursuing. That preparation should help you to feel calmer on the day, but even the best-prepared candidates can let the pressure of the big event dent their confidence. There are a number of tips and tricks you can use to fight such demons, but before you try any of them, it's important you cultivate a base of self-acceptance. If you're shy, accept the fact. (Presumably you're not applying to be a TV presenter.) Remind yourself why your character and background make you a good fit for this job. Be proud that you have already overcome a huge hurdle to be invited to interview. The company has asked to see you today because they want to meet *you*, not some cartoon version of the confident professional. The fundamental basis of confidence is simply being yourself and knowing yourself. Start there.

Now, about those tips and tricks

Let's be honest, even if your head is in the right place and your preparation is impeccable, your body can let you down. In high-pressure situations our bodies' natural 'flight or fight' response kicks in: you sweat, your mouth goes dry, your hands start to shake, your mind goes foggy and your stomach fills with butterflies. When you're in this sort of condition, it's hard to remember and confidently deliver the answers you thought about so carefully earlier.

When it comes to the physical effects of nerves, fight fire with fire. Your body can affect your state of mind in good ways as well as bad. Social psychologist and body-language expert Amy Cuddy has studied how our posture can change our body chemistry and our confidence. 'It goes both ways,' Cuddy explains. 'When you pretend to be powerful, you are more likely to actually feel more powerful. We know that our minds change our bodies, but it's also true that our bodies change our minds.' Cuddy discovered that holding what she terms 'power poses' – spreading yourself out like an alpha gorilla or Wonder Woman – for just two minutes can actually lower the amount of the stress hormone cortisol in the body by 25 per cent.

It might make you feel a bit silly but take a few minutes before your interview to sit quietly and stretch out and expand yourself like you're the king or queen of the world. Overcome your embarrassment and spend just two minutes focusing yourself, breathing deeply and practising your power pose. Clenching and unclenching various parts of your body can also help to release stress and relieve the symptoms of anxiety. If you have a smartphone or other gadget on you, paying a quick visit to your favourite humour site is, for once, not a form of procrastination. Making yourself laugh ahead of an interview – even if it's with silly cat pictures or bad internet jokes – has been shown to relieve physiological tension.

Of course, all this will work a lot better if you come to the interview well rested and not overly caffeinated. Hopefully, you don't need to be told that is essential to try to get a good night's sleep before your interview (and on the penultimate night too – some studies have shown that that has the most beneficial impact) and to keep your morning coffees to a reasonable number. Many candidates find that getting some exercise the day before the interview – or even the morning of it if scheduling permits – helps them feel more physically relaxed. Also, make sure you eat something (skip the garlic!) before you head out, so your stomach isn't distracting you, or the interviewer, with its rumbling.

....

Many interviewers are themselves new to the process and/or nervous about their own performance.

....

You are likely not to be the only one suffering from nerves. Keep in mind that your mental image of those across the table from you as powerful, competent and collected can be completely at odds with reality.

Focusing on the other performers on stage is a tried and true method for actors to battle stage fright, and it can also work for candidates. Pay attention to the emotional state of the interviewer and try to set them at ease. Not only will this give you something else to focus on rather than yourself, which in itself is likely to ease your anxiety, but it also makes it more likely you'll achieve a genuine human connection – and that should be the ultimate aim of any candidate.

Meeting the interviewer

We'd all like to believe that the world is fair and rational, but research (and experience) indicates that it's not. This is true of interviews too. First impressions matter . . . *a lot*. Study after study underlines this point. One found that a third of hiring managers decide whether to hire someone within ninety seconds of meeting them. Another found students could predict with great accuracy whether a candidate would get a job just by observing the first fifteen seconds of an interview. Fifteen seconds! That's basically just a handshake and hello. Nick Keeley, director of the careers service at Newcastle University told the *Guardian* that 'three-quarters of interviews are failed within three minutes of entering the room'.

What's worse, once we make an impression it's hard to change it. Studies suggest that even if later information firmly contradicts a first impression in interview, we are highly reluctant to change our opinion. Put all these studies together and they add up to one simple conclusion – you need to be on your best form from the moment you step into the building of a potential employer until the moment you walk out the door.

Yes, the receptionist is likely to notice if you opt for *Hello!* magazine rather than *The Economist* while you wait to be called into the interview, and the hiring manager is very likely to ask the receptionist if you were polite to everyone you met. Body language matters too. Are you sitting there fidgeting, slouching or otherwise letting your nerves show? Stop immediately. When you meet people, make sure you make eye contact and remember everyone's name. Obviously, you don't want to smell of cigarettes or half a bottle of aftershave. And make sure your mobile is switched off.

What about the old saw about a firm handshake? Turns out that one is scientifically validated too. One study had independent evaluators rank the quality of candidates' handshakes. A good, firm (but not crushing) handshake, the researchers discovered, is highly correlated to interviewer hiring recommendations.

The dress-code minefield

The most stressful aspect of making a good impression, however, is usually choosing what to wear. With standards varying not only from industry to industry but also company to company, it can seem like an impossible task to get it right.

But the issue is simpler than it first appears. No matter what type of role you're interviewing for, one rule applies: wear an outfit that is just slightly more formal than what you'd wear day-to-day on the job or expect your interviewer to wear. So if you're interviewing at a buttoned-up bank, you obviously need to be in your best suit. If you're trying to get a job at a start-up where everyone comes to work in T-shirts and jeans then wear your best pair of jeans and a slightly smarter shirt.

What if you're not sure about the day-to-day dress code at the company? The internet is your friend. A quick glance at their web page may give you some idea. If you're truly stumped, why not swing by the building one lunch hour and watch people coming and going to get an idea? Don't forget to take the weather into account as well – profuse sweating or shivering has never helped anyone make a great first impression.

Whatever you decide to wear, make sure you make your selection the night before to avoid stress on the day. Your outfit should be clean, wrinkle free and, don't forget, comfortable as well. Women should generally keep their makeup and accessories simple. Also, take the sit test. Do you look and feel as good sitting down as you did standing up? You'll probably spend the vast majority of your interview in a chair so this is important.

Taking the time to choose an outfit that shows effort and

makes you feel confident is likely to pay dividends not only when it comes to your demeanour and confidence level, but also in the interviewer's assessment of your competence. A phenomenon known as the 'halo effect' means that when we have a positive opinion of someone in one area – their dress sense, say – we tend to view them positively in other unrelated areas such as competence and personality. Take advantage of this fact.

Interview questions and the interviewers who love them

The Six Cs

There are hundreds of interview questions doing the rounds out there, but don't be intimidated by their variety: nearly all of them resolve into one of a few broad themes. If you can understand these themes, you'll find it easier to prepare an answer in advance or, if needed, to improvise your way to a good answer on the spot.

I call these themes the 'Six Cs':

- Classic questions (the 'Fateful 15')
- Career goal questions
- Character questions
- Competency questions
- Curveball questions
- Creativity questions

The main section of this book is organized around the Six Cs, and a category summary opens each chapter.

Rogues' gallery of interviewers

Finally, before we begin in earnest, here's a (slightly) tongue-in-cheek gallery of interviewers that you might meet on your travels. You probably won't encounter anyone in quite the exaggerated form depicted here, but every interviewer can show flashes of these traits, so the next time you meet one in the wild, don't feel unlucky. Interviewing is difficult and some people are better at it than others. That's something you should accept from the outset, certainly if you want to come across as a team player. Nevertheless, it helps to know in advance that interviewing makes people on both sides of the table say and do odd things. What follows is a list of odd traits that interviewers have been known to adopt:

The unicorn hunter

Characteristics: The perfect candidate doesn't exist, but that doesn't deter the unicorn hunter from looking.
Good points: They know what kind of candidate they want. Namely, one who's good at everything.
Bad points: Never quite finds the candidate they want, naturally; prone to nitpicking. Rarely makes people feel good about themselves.
Your tactics: Get them to specifically state the competencies required and show how you meet them; constantly suggest the natural trade-offs in your skills and experiences in order to demonstrate the widest range of your good points.

The late-running runaway train

Characteristics: Tumbles in to the room thirty minutes late, owing to three back-to-back interviews that morning. Is not fully in control of their inbox, diary, desk, life . . . you name it, they're not in control of it.

Good points: Hasn't had time to notice the gaps in your CV; is even more nervous and ill-prepared than you.

Bad points: Doesn't know who they're talking to, and might be too busy to remember – unless you wow them.

Your tactics: Since they're 'winging it', they will gladly let you do the talking, so *talk*. Be effusive and expansive. Show good manners, patience and positivity. Josh the whole thing along.

Method man/woman

Characteristics: Asks every candidate exactly the same questions and in the same order. Loves competency questions. Commonly found in the public sector and very large companies.

Good points: Is often a consummate professional, underneath it all. If they can tick a box, you're in.

Bad points: Doesn't give much encouragement; does a bad job of selling the organization to you.

Your tactics: Look for competencies on the job description and point them out on your CV – twice.

Napoleon

Characteristics: Usually male. Is proud of his many achievements. Does all the talking, but asks no questions. May bring along a silent and junior colleague whose presence is not explained.

Good points: Responds to flattery and questions.

Bad points: Prefers yes-men; hasn't been rejected or criticized in a long time. Wants you to be as personally loyal to them as to the company.

Your tactics: Offer praise whenever you mean it, and silence when you don't.

The suitor

Characteristics: Known to hire attractive people.
Good points: Finds you attractive.
Bad points: Is looking for love in all the wrong places. Prone to innuendo. The male of the species will often scare off good female candidates.
Your tactics: Move on, not in.

The B player

Characteristics: The B player likes to hire C players.
Good points: Is keen to teach you, on account of your junior status here.
Bad points: Might actually be a C player, and may prefer you to stay their junior for ever.
Your tactics: Give away your ideas freely. Turn up the volume on your personal strengths and professional achievements. It might cost you the job, but you deserve better anyway.

The dues-payer

Characteristics: Defines success in terms of their career path, and their path only. Not keen on career-switchers.
Good points: Is usually a genuine expert on something. Their skills will complement your own, not vie with them.
Bad points: 'I spent twenty years coming up through the marketing department. Why haven't you?'
Your tactics: Compliment their talents, and show how your skills are really just another manifestation of theirs.

The RHINO (Really Here In Name Only)

Characteristics: Pleasant enough, but doesn't seem to apply themselves to the interview. It's as though he or she has already given the job to someone else.

Good points: Asks gentle questions, lots of small talk.

Bad points: They really *have* given the job to someone else.

Your tactics: Even if you feel it's hopeless, put on the best show you can. Be gracious: the RHINO might get you a job elsewhere at the company. In any case, some RHINOs are really just method men/women, plodding on without thinking to encourage you.

The entrepreneur

Characteristics: Founder and sole owner of the company.

Good points: Above-average energy and IQ, else they wouldn't have survived long enough to employ you.

Bad points: 'You want *how much*?' Also, is often a nutcase.

Your tactics: Play up your work ethic, your loyalty and your flexibility – but only if you're genuinely feeling all those things. If not, don't work for an entrepreneur.

The poker player

Characteristics: Is often the CEO, or will be. A warm and genuine exterior conceals inner steel.

Good points: Expert interviewer and team builder. Effortlessly charming. Knows everyone. Makes you want to work there.

Bad points: With their supreme poker face, you may never know if you said the wrong thing.

Your tactics: Ask not what your employer can do for you . . . just focus on showing what you can do for them.

. . . and finally . . .

Goldilocks

Characteristics: Neither too cold nor too warm.

Good points: Never puts a foot wrong; wants you to be yourself, gives good feedback.

Bad points: Rarely seen in the wild, or so says the unicorn hunter.

Your tactics: If you meet one, pat yourself on the back for bringing out the best in people.

TWO

CLASSIC INTERVIEW QUESTIONS: THE 'FATEFUL 15'

I've collected together these fifteen classic questions partly because they form the basis of almost every other interview question, but also because my research suggests that these are the fifteen questions you're most likely to be asked. So, if you're pushed for time you can go a long way – though not all the way – by preparing an answer for these fifteen alone.

Some 'how-to-interview' books would have you believe that you will be asked one of *several hundred* interview questions, all fundamentally different. My view is that there are only a limited number of valid, distinct questions to contend with. More practically, I also believe that while every candidate must choose where their preparation ends, every candidate ought to *start* their preparation with these fifteen classics. That's not just because these are the questions most likely to be headed your way – it's also because interviewers demand a higher quality of answer for the simple, classic questions such as *Tell me about yourself* than they do for the more zany questions like *What animal would you be?* Your interviewer might be delighted to hear you'd rather be an otter than a dolphin, but they're certainly more keen to know why you're a good fit for the job in question. If you've been reading those books that insist you prepare answers for hundreds of interview questions, chances are you're firmly into dolphin and otter territory. My view is that you're better off focusing on the Fateful 15 and working outwards from there, as energy and time permit.

1. Tell me about yourself

The Real Question: Who do you think you are? And will you know what to leave in and what to leave out?

Top-line Tactic: *Break it down, rehearse it, breeze it.*

We'll spend quite a bit of time on this question, because no other can pull the rug from under you as fast.

Why this question causes so much difficulty

In common with all open-ended questions, there is no obvious answer to *Tell me about yourself*. It's all on you to choose what to say and when to stop saying it.

The question is a very reliable measure of a candidate's self-confidence and their degree of preparation, for two reasons. First, the less confident and prepared candidates typically begin by asking for further clarification, before ending their response with a request for endorsement, i.e. they start with *Do you want me to tell you about professional stuff or personal stuff?* and end with *Um . . . is that what you were looking for?* Neither sounds great to the average interviewer.

Second, we all have weaknesses and we all know that we shouldn't mention them in interview. But once you start thinking about the topic of what you shouldn't think about, you're almost doomed to start talking about it too. When an interviewer says, *Tell me about yourself*, by implication you're being asked *not* to dwell on all your weaknesses as a candidate. At that point, it's very common for your mind to start dwelling on nothing else *but* your weaknesses – to start talking about that time you got fired, or your poor health, maybe even your *Star Trek* figurine collection.

The human brain can only do one task at a time, but this question tries to make it perform two: working out what to say *and* what not to say. Keeping those two tasks in mind is hard work in the heat of an interview, especially since most of us are essentially honest and most of us are a little self-conscious. Sometimes your mind tries to reduce its workload by flushing everything out at once. That's why almost every interviewer has seen a candidate make an unforced confession.

So what to do? The best way is to rehearse your own structure and – crucially – to impose it without asking, as if your individual approach to answering open questions is the most natural thing in the world.

Almost any structure will do, as long as you know what it is and have rehearsed it many times. Here are a few suggested structures for *Tell me about yourself*:

Structure: Professional summary and goals

*I'm a **chief operating officer** with fifteen years' experience in residential property, **looking to move into the CEO role** for a public-listed estate agency.*

Structure: Movie plot

*After **university** I started out in **finance**, but I **discovered** that my **true love** was in fact **computer programming**. I made the **switch** five years ago and I **haven't looked back**. Now I'm looking to take on a big role at an IT firm with clients in the City.*

Structure: Roles and hobbies

*I'm a registered **nurse**, a **father** of three – and a **ski bum** when I get the chance.*

Structure: Affiliations

*I'm a **Canadian** living in **Brighton**, working in the **financial sector**. At weekends I do voluntary work on behalf of **homeless people**.*

Catchy sequence

*I always say I've had **three** careers, **two** kids, **one** husband and **no** regrets.*

End with a perceptible flourish, so as to hand back control to the interviewer. Please note that asking, 'Is that enough?' is not a definite flourish: it's a cry for help. A better way to signal an end is to mirror the interviewer's language in the original question.

. . . and that, to answer your question, is a little bit about me.

If you find the above approach is a little too sing-song for you, here are some waypoints for an alternative approach.

1. You need to show a logical progression or underlying theme – you need to tell a story, in other words.
2. You need to flag that you know exactly what you're going to say and that it won't take long. ('Tell you about myself? Sure. I'll give you the sixty-second version to start with; let me know if you want any more.') Whatever you do, don't sound like you've never been asked the question before and so are about to start introspecting there and then. You should have done *that* before you got in the car, as parents of small children like to say. And make sure you know what you're going to say if the interviewer *does* ask for more.

3. Don't ask whether they want personal or professional stuff: that's not what confident people do. Make the content of your biographical summary 90 per cent professional and 10 per cent personal. It's a business meeting, not a date.

4. Your story needn't have a definite beginning, especially if you're a more experienced candidate, but it will need a definite 'middle' that makes clear what you've been up to lately and how that is feeding into your skills and experience, and how in turn your skills and experience feed into the job on offer.

5. You'll also need a definite 'ending' to show that you've stopped talking and are handing back to the interviewer. A brief reference to your social life and interests will suffice here.

6. Feel free to leap back and forth in time – start with your job title, then regress to whatever start point you choose and work forward again, to show a logical progression that *goes past your current job title* to explain your interest in the vacancy, and your suitability for it.

7. You are not your job title, yet this is one time when it can be useful in setting you off on your answer. Starting with your current job title makes you sound brisk and businesslike: 'I'm currently an assistant marketing manager for Tesco' might not be as lyrical a start as 'I'm a woman who loves working in retail grocery', but nor does it sound like your conversation is about to go wandering aimlessly around the room, which is always the risk with this question. (By the way, 'I'm a recent graduate looking for a first job in law' is a job title too, and a pretty good one compared to what most of your peers usually say when asked the same question.)

8. Some people view this question as an opportunity to start talking about their strengths and weaknesses, but there's

an equally good argument for just sticking to your professional achievements and passions instead. The latter view holds that, for this question, your true personal strengths ought to emerge not from your mouth but from your results. Your interviewer will almost certainly ask about your strengths later on, so you can save the explicit superlatives for then.

9. Finish on a pertinent but uncontroversial question (see 'New World wines' in the example below).

Bringing all that together:

As you know, I'm an assistant marketing manager for T——, specializing in wines and spirits, and I've been in the industry eight years.

I come from Durham. My family have several shops there, which is probably why I was attracted to this line of work.

I studied retail management at Nottingham University, which was great. I found grocery management particularly interesting, and went for a summer internship for S—— that I really enjoyed.

My first full-time job was with T——, as a buyer on the homeware section. I didn't know much about homeware when I started, but I managed to double sales year on year and won the store's employee of the year award. That got me promotion to head office as an assistant marketing manager, working in wines and spirits, which is where I am now.

The job you're offering is the next logical career move. I enjoy working in wines and spirits, and I think I'd be a good fit here. I believe you're looking to improve your sales of New World wines, aren't you? [You've researched this, so you know it's correct.] *So that would be the first area I'd concentrate on.*

Outside work, I enjoy outdoor pursuits. I like skiing especially. [You can add a sentence here about your family or partner, if you have one.] *I blog about wines and spirits as well.*

Is there anything else you'd like to know?

Setting the tone

In researching this book, one Reed recruiter told us that the candidate's enthusiasm and energy when answering *Tell me about yourself* usually sets the tone for the rest of the interview, *in terms of the interviewer's enjoyment of it*. If someone is timid in answering this question, the interviewer is very likely to have a heart-sink moment. Interviewers are people too: it's kind of soul-destroying for them to be forced to spend an entire day in a windowless interview room with a procession of people who can't speak with any gusto. As interviewers see it, if you can't answer this question in a way that makes you sound like you're going to be a fun person to spend the next sixty minutes with, chances are no other question will bring you out of your shell.

Most people will take you at your own estimation when answering *Tell me about yourself*, so watch out for false modesty, false bravado – false *anything*. Speak without the usual self-deprecation or puffery that's typical of everyday conversations. You're on stage here.

Places, everybody!

Finally, there are some interview questions where sounding rehearsed will count against you, and others where rehearsal is essential to avoid petering out or wandering into a minefield.

Tell me about yourself is a rehearser, for sure.

If you don't agree, try answering it right now, off the cuff, and see how well you do. Go on, *Tell me about yourself*.

2. Why are you applying?

The Real Question: What can you do that we need you to do? Do you even know what we need you to do?

Top-line Tactic: *Reflect the job spec in every line of your answer. Talk about their needs before you mention your own.*

The good thing about this question is that it lets you give the interviewer any number of reasons why you're right for the job. As such, you should welcome it – but many candidates don't. That's because the question is also a huge, wide-open prairie in which anyone who makes up an answer on the spot is likely to get lost. And people who don't really enjoy their work also tend to struggle with this one too.

Happily, this seemingly daunting question happens to have a straightforward answer. The only thing the interviewer really wants to hear is this:

I'm applying because my **skills**, **experience** and **motivation** are the **best fit for the job**.

. . . and if the art of winning a job can be expressed in a single sentence, it would be that one. Here's what it might look like in longer form:

When I read the job ad, I could see straight away the fit between what you're looking for and what I've done in my career to date. That's also what I want to do much more of in future.

I've enjoyed my time at B―― but, with my experience in aerodynamics, I know I can make a bigger contribution at A――.

Also, I like the way you do things here. [Give an example.] *If I ran an airline, I'd certainly buy an A— over a B—.*

It's well known that A— is a good employer and you have a terrific corporate social responsibility programme – but mainly I'm applying because I think I can do this job very well, and have fun doing it.

The good thing about this answer is that it implies long-term satisfaction all round. Sure, you can move jobs for a bigger salary, and people often do, but all the evidence is that the thrill of a bigger salary fades quickly. That's why 'more money' is never a good reason to take a job, at least not as far as the employer is concerned. Conversely, a person's *values* tend to be stable and enduring, so someone who cares about corporate social responsibility today is likely to care about it ten years from now. In the example above, the candidate has been careful to point out that their personal values align with the firm's values.

Of course, some things in life don't need saying, including:

- Everyone needs an income.
- It's nice to get out of the house.
- A short commute is better than a long one.

. . . and since they don't need saying, you won't be bringing them up in answer to *Why are you applying?* will you?

As with all of our Fateful 15 questions, if you can reflect upon what you really want from your job and what it is that you have to offer, you'll be able to improvise your way through this question and almost any other.

3. What are your greatest strengths?

The Real Question: Do you really know yourself – and do you know what our problem is here?

Top-line Tactic: *Answer with the job description uppermost in mind. Go easy on the adjectives and heavy on hard data.*

We all carry in our heads a vague list of our personal strengths. This list is usually a few years old, hardly changes over time and is often a mixture of facts and wishes. This dusty old list is what many of us resort to when asked in interview for our strengths, when really what's needed is a much newer list of strengths – the list where you've thought hard about this particular job's key requirements and mapped them against your best achievements to date. *That* list is the only one that's going to win them over.

To repeat an earlier point, you're there to solve the employer's problems. You're not there to make people think you're smart, nice or generally a good, professional all-rounder. All those things may be necessary, but they're not sufficient. You must go beyond listing pleasant-sounding adjectives such as 'hard-working' and 'trustworthy'. So many people think that choosing the right adjective is the key to answering this question – but adjectives can't solve the employer's problems. Adjectives can't put up shelves, write marketing plans or drive a fork-lift truck. You need to provide hard examples, with dates, characters and numbers.

In choosing which strength to talk about, see if you can veer towards aspects of yourself that fit into a decent plotline, something that shows progression and development over time. (It's hard to weave an interesting story about you being merely hard-working and trustworthy.)

Start with an adjective to describe your strength, sure, but only to lead your audience in. Straight after your adjective, explain the context in which that strength was used, starting with your most recent role, describe the impact of your strength, and give it some basic dramatic elements, e.g. what was started, stopped or transformed as a result. Also, give an instance where your strengths were acknowledged by others – just so the interviewer knows it isn't all in your mind.

....

A note about tone

With some questions more than others, how you answer is just as important as what you say. For example, for any job involving leadership skills you'll need to convey personal authority without also sounding boorish or, more commonly, like you believe you're not really up to it. Obviously practice will help here, but nothing beats sitting down with a good (i.e. honest) friend and using their ears to check your pitch. Your friend won't know whether you believe what you're saying or not, but they will be able to hear it in your voice and tell you whether you sound like you mean it.

....

Since outlining your strengths is the number one task in interview, you should not wait to be asked the exact question as phrased here. Other questions call for exactly the same answer, such as *Why are you a good fit for this company? and Why should we hire you?*

Market trends! I've always been very good at reading market trends and staying in step with them. It's something that comes naturally to me, something that other people recognize I'm good at – and something I pride myself on, too.

To give you an example, out of all the fashion buyers in my industry I was the first to realize that our stores could make money from selling mobile phone accessories – even though we're principally a fashion retailer. I saw early on that young people might buy mobile phone cases as fashion accessories, with different colours to match different outfits and so on. My manager usually trusts me on trend spotting so she let me experiment and now our technology line is the fastest growing category in the store.

It's had a great impact on the company, because it put people in the mood to experiment with other technology lines – so now we're doing well with things like headphones too. I think my success at spotting trends is why they promoted me to chief buyer. Now I'm responsible for helping other buyers develop their trend-spotting skills – and I'm certain I could bring those training skills to this job too.

4. What are your greatest weaknesses?

The Real Question: Am I right in thinking X about you? And are you going to give me the same old evasive and lame answers that everybody else did, or are you going to level with me?

Top-line Tactic: *If you've been invited for interview, chances are that the interviewer is seeking affirmation of predicted weaknesses, not information about new ones.*

There is no quicker way to break the rapport between you and your interviewer than to give a clichéd answer to this question, or to pretend, as many do, that your weaknesses are trivial and irrelevant.

As Barack Obama found out, when the time comes to answer the dreaded 'weaknesses question' the golden rule is to *actually answer the question*, dammit.

When you have nuclear launch codes, your personal weaknesses really matter. If you pretend they don't matter, you should expect a seasoned interviewer to pull you up. That's exactly what TV news reporter Katie Couric did to Obama during the 2008 US presidential election campaign.

COURIC: What one personal flaw do you think might hinder your ability to be president?

OBAMA: I think that all of us have things we need to improve. You know, I have said that my management of paper can sometimes be a problem.

COURIC: You can come up with something better than that, though, can't you?

Bang! *You can come up with something better than that.* Regardless of personal politics, anyone watching might have cheered when they saw this well-worn canned answer shot down in flames. No one likes to be finessed.

So many people dodge this question in interview; it is very frustrating for interviewers when it happens. Some interviewers will show their frustration, some won't, but all will feel it. Couric wasn't going to let the candidate mumble something about paperwork, and you should assume you won't be allowed to either.

So when your interviewer asks what you think your weaknesses are, it's best to level with them. If you don't, your interviewer probably won't let you get away with it, just as Couric didn't let Obama get away with it.

To be fair to Obama, he managed to pull his interview back on track with a good follow-up answer, one in which he successfully reminds us all that strengths and weaknesses are usually two sides of the same coin. Funnily enough, Obama in office gathered a reputation for being either a careful thinker or a slow decision maker – pick one according to your personal politics – so it is interesting to see that same theme emerge in his answer prior to election.

I use paperwork as an example of something that I'm constantly tryin' to work on. What is often a strength can be a weakness. So, you know, for me there are times where I want to think through all our options. At some point you've gotta make sure that we're making a decision. So far, at least I've proven to be pretty good about knowing when that time is. I think, as president, with all the information that's coming at you constantly, you're never gonna have 100 per cent information. And you've just gotta make the call quickly and surely.

With these words, he answered the question with a real example of what could be seen as a weakness – and he still got the job.

All the same, don't make the interviewer ask this question twice, like Couric had to. Your first answer should always leave the interviewer wholly satisfied. Here's how you can do that and remain attractive to them:

- Tell them what they already know. There's a good chance the interviewer already has a few ideas about your weaknesses and is keen to have those ideas confirmed or contextualized. And if you've done your homework, the lean patches in your CV (relating to the job description) will be just as apparent to you as to them – so those lean patches should be exactly what you address. By sticking only to weaknesses apparent on your CV, you'll avoid introducing a new monster-under-the-bed that the interviewer hadn't spotted.
- Make it abundantly clear you know what your weaknesses are, and that they don't perturb *you*. Answer like you're giving

your name and address, not a forced confession. Speak with the confidence of someone who knows that their weakness isn't going to be a deal-breaker (if it were a deal-breaker, you probably wouldn't be sitting there in the first place).

- Cite evidence to show you're working on your weaknesses. A life-long learner is better suited to today's rapidly changing workplace than someone born with a natural but narrow talent that they rest on.

- Talking about gaps in your CV is a lot less subjective and disaster-prone than talking about what you or others see as moral failings in your *character*. For example, the difference between stubbornness and persistence is nearly always in the eye of the beholder. You've probably no idea whether the interviewer rates you as stubborn or persistent, nor are you likely to change their mind with mere talk, so don't worry about drawing fine distinctions of character. Just stick to talking about the job description, your skills and your career history.

- Most jobs measure you against a series of key performance indicators (KPIs). Some of these will be most important (e.g. how many cars you sold last month), some will be less important (e.g. how many blue cars you sold last month). You will impress the interviewer if your answer to the weakness question directly references your KPIs, because that will show you keep your eye on what the company thinks is important. Also, most people *wouldn't dare* answer this question with reference to KPIs, and that's your opportunity to score highly on honesty and integrity. Just make sure you're talking about a lesser KPI.

End your answer by asking a question, in order to get the conversation back to what you *can* do. It wouldn't hurt to ask if you've addressed their concerns.

Above all, stop thinking that there is a right answer to this question. If you're looking for a potted answer that works in all weathers, you have the wrong mindset.

With that in mind, you need never again utter any of the following mealy-mouthed, semi-dishonest canned weaknesses, such as:

- I'm a perfectionist [Whatever you do, don't say this: it's been done to death.]
- I work too hard/care too much.
- I get frustrated when colleagues don't pull their weight.
- I get lost in the details.
- I don't have any!
- Chocolate.
- I'm not good at [something the job obviously doesn't require].

These are poor answers because they sound insincere – and because none shows any evidence that you've considered your CV against the job description. In other words, you're not talking to the employer about helping them with their problem. You're just talking about yourself, and doing so in a vague and dissembling fashion.

Here's all the foregoing advice wrapped up in a demo answer:

I'd say that my greatest weakness so far as you're concerned is that I've been out of the workforce for a couple of years in order to raise my family. I didn't drop out of the industry altogether during that time, though. My contacts book is up to date and I've kept up with industry trends. For example, I enrolled for online professional development courses with [give examples]. That's something I wouldn't have had time to do if I'd been at work, so in a way being out of the workforce has done me some good. Also, I'm a regular on most of the [industry name] *blogs and forums.*

If you take me on, I certainly don't think I'll need retraining.

In my last job, our KPIs measured all things great and small, and I didn't hit every target I was set, so that's perhaps a weakness. I did hit all the KPIs that counted the most, though.

Was there anything on my CV that especially concerned you?

5. What will your skills and ideas bring to this company?

The Real Question: What will we be buying from you?

Top-line Tactic: *You can appear generous or miserly – and no one wants a miser.*

In answering this question, you may well feel you're running the risk of giving away your ideas for free.

Whenever an interviewer asks you to volunteer your know-how, there's always the feeling that they'll steal your ideas without hiring you, and maybe cackle like Dr Evil into the bargain.

It happens. Some companies, many of them large enough to know better, do indeed pick up ideas for free wherever they can get them, including circumstances in which the originator might expect to be paid. There are many words to describe this practice, including 'despicable' and 'cheap'.

But another word for it is 'life'.

As any patent lawyer will tell you after a few drinks, ideas are two a penny and very few of them can be 100 per cent protected against copying. To have an idea is to risk losing it to the crowd, and there's little anyone can do about it.

So, when the interviewer asks for a few ideas, as many of them will, it is best to err on the side of openness and enthusiasm. Don't worry if your ideas are not a perfect match for what they want or what they do – if they like you, they'll probably chalk up those mistakes to your outsider status. The important thing is to be effusive, and to show that you think of the hiring firm in terms of having problems and opportunities that could benefit from your help.

Also, you should present your ideas in terms of previous work that you have executed *personally* – because execution counts just as much as ideas. For example, a sandwich bar is not a terribly innovative idea, and when the founders of Pret A Manger first went into business, London was not short of such outlets. But what London lacked was a sandwich bar *done well*, and done by the sort of people prepared to try harder than everyone else. Scoring highly on drive and execution will make you much more bankable than a person with superior ideas who doesn't deliver.

Above all, it stands to reason that someone with an idea worth stealing is, on the face of it, someone worth employing. So, when they ask this question, take the plunge and show them what you're made of.

6. What's your preferred management style?

The Real Question: Are you and I going to get on?

Top-line Tactic: *Aim to be the boss and the subordinate you always wanted for yourself, even if nobody's perfect.*

If there's any justice in the world, we should manage colleagues the same way we like to be managed ourselves. That's why it's worth considering the two topics – of managing and being managed – as one.

Very often the person interviewing you is going to be your future boss, so it's almost inevitable they'll ask what you do and don't like in a manager. And it's a good sign they do: a David Brent boss wouldn't think to ask and a Genghis Khan boss wouldn't care to.

The blueprint for answering this question is predictable enough. Bosses want to see someone who can work under their own steam but who also recognizes that a workplace is hierarchical. Bosses want to feel that their style of communication is such that they can brief you to do the job without actually spelling it all out for you. Bosses want to hear that you are always prepared to take good and bad news with equally good grace, and that, perhaps as a manager yourself, you can give out bad news with respect and humility, and give off enough good energy to pep the troops.

And if it feels as though the average boss wants the moon on a plate, it's important to remember that your boss's management style was probably shaped in childhood and that you're not about to change it anytime soon. Even if you don't accept a job offer from that person, you do have to accept their management style. If you have very precise needs about being managed, it's not a good idea to tease out those needs in every last detail at your interview, as there is an assumption that your boss is the boss, like it or not. They're buying, you're selling. If you really want to know what that person is going to be like as your boss, get on LinkedIn and find one of your interviewer's former co-workers: they'll probably enjoy telling you. Don't try to find out too much about them in interview.

Future Boss will also want to see you have some degree of sympathy with their trials and tribulations as a manager. After all, managing people can be a thankless experience – too many subordinates forget that.

Rolling all that into a sample answer:

Good question. I think that half the trick of managing people is not being scared to ask them what they think – like you've just asked me.

It seems to me that being a boss is straightforward in principle. It's about clear goals, clear communication and clear rewards. Ideally, I'd like a boss who knows when to intervene and when to let me get on with it, but obviously we won't always agree about that, which is as it should be.

It's not easy, being a boss, I appreciate that. You have to lead by example, even when you're not sure what the best thing to do is, and you're going to get it wrong occasionally. I don't expect perfection in a boss, but I do like one with a sense of humour when things don't go to plan, and that goes for the team as well.

It wouldn't hurt to talk about key moments in your experience of being a subordinate or a manager, most notably involving issues of conflict, success, goal setting and staff performance.

7. Where do you see yourself in five years' time?

The Real Question: Are you after this job or just any job? How soon will you need a new challenge? Do you have a realistic sense of what we can offer you?

Top-line Tactic: *If you don't know, calmly say so, as if not knowing were the most natural thing in the world – because it is.*

This question is both highly popular and, for some, exceedingly difficult to answer.

If you're one of those superhuman types with a well-mapped-out career plan, one that doesn't sound too prescriptive and presumptuous, then by all means wheel that plan out when you're asked this question.

Everybody else – i.e. most of us – should give themselves permission to not have the faintest idea where they'll be in five years' time. It's perfectly normal and OK to not know. And if you make inner peace with not knowing, you will be on your way to giving a good answer.

One way to answer honestly is to acknowledge out loud that you're there to talk about the job on offer, not the job it leads to. Also, use the opportunity to detail your achievements to date, before saying you'd hope to be equally successful at this company.

Employers may not expect to hear ruthless or driving ambition. 'I want to be doing your job!' is usually an instant fail – for many interviewers it's far too confrontational. If you want to show a desire to progress then you may prefer to say:

I don't know your company well enough to say exactly, but I'd like to think I'll be working here in whatever capacity I'm best suited to.

This shows the interviewer that you're there primarily to make a contribution to the company, that you're not just in it for what you can get. Also, there's never any harm in reminding them what drew you to the company in the first place:

It's common knowledge that your company has the highest programming standards and the best software engineers in the industry, so if that's still the case five years from now, I hope I'll be working here.

For certain roles it may be more desirable that the candidate wants to be doing the same job without any particular desire for promotion or development. In this case you should play up your loyalty to your employer and explain that in five years' time you hope still to be with the company and making a valuable contribution in the advertised post.

For younger candidates, five years is a long way off – long enough to start speculating about some alternate universe they'll be living in by then. Even though this question is intended to help the interviewer get to know the true you, your non-work dreams are at best irrelevant and, at worst, suggest an unfocused and footloose personality. Hence you should keep your plans to climb Kilimanjaro or start your own business under wraps.

Be honest about your drive and ambition, but make sure you temper it and demonstrate that you are realistic about your prospects. Map out a tentative travel plan for the next five years, and the principles by which you will reach your desired destination, rather than just stating where you're heading. Here's a good mindset, especially for recent grads:

Five years from now I hope to have learned enough to be training other people, maybe managing them too – if the opportunity arises.

It can be a little hard to hand this one back, so always keep in mind your short, high-level summary of what the job is for.

A home nurse's job is all about helping patients get back on their feet after illness, so in five years I hope to still be doing that, one way or another – whether as a nurse in the field or a team leader in the office.

A good answer to this question will reveal a candidate who

knows how they hope to travel, if not necessarily exactly where they're going.

8. How would you approach this job?

The Real Question: How well do you know us? What's your take on what we need? What's your preferred style of working?

Top-line Tactic: *Talk about diplomacy before talking about your plans.*

Be careful here. This question may give you a chance to talk about your experience and skills that are relevant to the role, but you can't know how a company really functions until you've started working there – so don't be wrong-footed into making sweeping statements.

You can answer by referring to previous successes in your current job. Describe your way of working there and what you achieved, taking care to relate everything to the vacancy on offer. Say you'd like to replicate those successes if you are offered the role.

You can also use this question to show your ability to adapt to the company you hope to join. You should acknowledge that all companies are different, so you would use your first few weeks on the job to learn systems and get to know colleagues before creating your departmental plan. This will show the interviewer that you are planning for success in the new role but that you don't have a completely rigid idea of how the company should operate.

Well, the best way to do this job won't become clear until I join the company, so the first thing I'll be doing is getting to know my colleagues, listening, taking notes, building relationships, helping them out where I can. And it never hurts to ask colleagues what they're expecting from me. I'd also hope my manager will tell me about the unwritten rules and conventions here – every workplace has some of those.

After I've done all that I'll be able to come up with a plan of action. In my last job I got good results by . . .

9. What have you achieved elsewhere?

The Real Question: What's the very best that we can expect from you? Is it what we need?

Top-line Tactic: *Keep it recent, work-related and well-rehearsed. Permit yourself to sound confident – they want you to be.*

Good news, everybody! You've just obtained temporary clearance to blow your own trumpet.

Too bad, then, that so few people are capable of articulating what makes them different from the other candidates, let alone better. Many people assume that their CV alone can adequately convey their achievements – but that presupposes the interviewer has had time to read your CV before the interview, when many interviewers are just too busy.

Also, most of us are just too modest. Our well-meaning parents have raised us to ensure we play nicely with others, and not to be too egotistical. That's why so many candidates find themselves at a loss when the time comes to talk uninterrupted about their greatest accomplishments. They don't realize that graceful self-promotion is often the key difference between career stagnation and career progression.

There are few things you can do to make talking about yourself feel natural. First, remember that the interviewer has willingly suspended the conversational niceties of modesty and subordination, and they've done so precisely because they want to hear about *the best version* of you.

Second, think of your achievements as a plotline rather than solely as a list of numbers or promotions. Don't be afraid to include dramatic effects such as jeopardy, doubt, conflict, growth and transformation. All those elements will bring the listener in, and you can see them at play in this sample answer:

I'd say my greatest achievement at work was last year's launch of W— snack bars. It's the first-ever health snack to sell a million units in the UK in under twelve months.

W— was well known in America but had no UK distribution. We weren't the strongest candidate to win the distribution deal, since both the company and I were relatively inexperienced, but W— had a product I believed in and I made that clear both to my directors and to W—.

W— gave me three months to make it work, saying that if I didn't get some traction in that time, they'd reassign the distribution rights to a rival firm.

Obviously, I hoped it wouldn't come to that, because that would have looked awful on my CV, but there were times when I thought it might. Sales were slow to start with, but I was determined to see it through. I just worked all hours and tried everything I could think of – I must have called literally hundreds of independent food shops trying to get them to stock W— products. It wasn't easy, but by doing that I got to know those customers a lot better and they got to know my company better too. Building those bridges is what really made the product take off. Plus, a lot of my customers discovered there was a good profit to be made from health products, which they hadn't realized before, so everyone was happy.

W— is my best achievement to date, not least because I've turned an underdog product into a household name. I couldn't have done that selling Coca-Cola or iPads.

Note the emphasis here on helping others achieve too.

There's nothing wrong with bringing screen-based evidence of your greatest accomplishments, but ask before you take out your tablet and, whatever you do, keep it super-short – five slides max, and number those slides 'one of five', etc., to reassure your interviewer that the presentation will be brief.

10. What did you like and dislike about your last job?

The Real Question: What do you want from us that the last lot couldn't give you? Can we give it to you?

Top-line Tactic: *Start with a long list of what makes you happy, then let them know that you don't expect perfection in any job.*

Let's start with what you didn't like about your last job. There's always something not to like, but the traditional advice is that it is never acceptable to bring it up in interview, because no one wants to hire a moaner.

But if you follow traditional advice here it will be very hard to sound sincere. For if you make your last job sound too good, it begs a further question about why you want to leave. And if it's so bad, how can you get that across without sounding too negative?

Of course, here the interviewer is *inviting* you to say something negative, on the assumption that we're all human and no job is perfect. Therefore, don't dodge the question – you really should talk about a few things you didn't enjoy. Just make sure that your answer demonstrates grit and a strong work ethic, one that can power through difficulties:

There was a lot about the job I enjoyed at my last company. I loved being out of the office, working on site, which put me in close contact with our customers and my colleagues. I felt like I was at the sharp end of the industry, in a way that I wouldn't have done sitting in an office.

But there were a few drawbacks. Being on site all the time often meant leaving home before breakfast and getting in after dark, so my family life was suffering. I had to do it, of course, in order to keep our promise of next-day service. I became so focused on the job that in the end I stopped thinking about the time of day. That's not really how I want to live.

I know the job I'm applying for will occasionally mean working unsocial hours, but I'm happy to accept that, since it's not something I'll be doing day in, day out.

Since you'll be articulating a few negative points, this question really does require you to make a careful inventory of your likes and dislikes long before you go into the interview room: you'll be sorry if you improvise that list on the spot.

Still stuck for inspiration? See if your current job offers you any of the following:

- meet interesting people
- opportunities for progress
- work independently
- atmosphere of trust, honesty and integrity
- overseas travel
- varied tasks
- constant learning
- requires or rewards creativity
- likeable co-workers
- face-to-face contact
- caring for others
- customer interaction

- clearly defined role
- close to management
- developing people
- positive impact on the community
- supportive culture
- playing with cool technology

11. Tell me about a time you worked in a team

The Real Question: No one achieves anything on their own – and you know that, right?

Top-line Tactic: *Find a recent, real-world example where you've played successfully with others.*

Unless you're applying to be the local hermit or lighthouse keeper, you will be assessed on your ability to work well with others. And of all the questions in our 'Fateful 15', it is this one which most closely follows the formula of a 'competency question'. You'll be hearing much more about competency questions later on; for now, please know that this formula of question requires that your answer be utterly truthful, concrete, specific, recent and focused on your actions. It should also end with a definite, positive outcome.

For this question in particular, the first step to a good answer is acknowledging the need to put in a *special effort* to make it memorable. That's because almost everyone is striving to come across as a team player: it can be hard to make your answer stand out.

Therefore, this is a perfect question to throw in a touch of colour or a quirky detail to differentiate your answer from a sea of 'I'm a great communicator' replies. Here's one example:

Last summer the company I'm currently working for relaunched its website with several important new features. It was a big project involving IT, several designers and marketing. My portion of the project – helping to develop a content-marketing strategy – was completed but a bug in the software accidentally deleted all the images for the redesign from the database the night before the big relaunch.

As you can imagine, it was pandemonium, but we all said we'd do whatever it took to fix it. Several of us from marketing were there half the night uploading the new pictures the designers had come up with while the IT people tried to fix the code – and we also ordered the pizzas to keep everyone going. I volunteered to keep management up to date on our progress to relieve some of the pressure on the technical team. We managed to get the website launched on time and traffic is now up more than 20 per cent after the redesign. Of course, it would have been better if that last-minute problem hadn't happened, but I actually feel the experience really bonded me to my teammates.

An answer like this ticks a couple of key boxes:

- It assigns credit where credit is due. Make sure you don't end up sounding like the type of person who steals the spotlight or undervalues others' contributions.
- It's memorable. Generic terms like 'team player' and 'effective communicator' go in one ear and out the other and don't sound particularly convincing. Anyone can rattle off buzzwords. People remember – and believe – concrete details like snack food and late nights far more easily.
- It illustrates key constituents of a good team player, like communication, adaptability, empathy and the ability to appreciate the perspective of others, and humour.

12. What do your co-workers say about you?

The Real Question: Do you sound calm or wary about this question? Are you self-aware or just self-conscious?

Top-line Tactic: *Testimonials, not adjectives.*

Some people are better at interviews than they are at actually doing any work. If that fact makes you despair, you'll be pleased to know that there's an antidote to those people. This question is that antidote.

There's no question quite like it for destabilizing people who haven't been telling the whole truth about their talents and their personality. That's why it's popular among recruiters, and definitely one you should include in your pre-interview training.

This question is destabilizing because an untruthful response requires multiple layers of deception – it's one thing to tell a fib about yourself, but quite another to put that fib into the mouth of an imaginary colleague who simply *loves* you and everything you do.

Unfortunately, it's also a question that trips up modest and unassuming types too, because they've been taught not to blow their horn and so are likely to do themselves down in order to give 'balance' to their answer.

And younger candidates are more likely to be tripped up by the question than older ones, simply because with age comes the realization that you can't please everyone. For this reason, younger candidates are more apt to give this question an anxious or overly strident response, whereas older candidates are much more likely to respond in a way that is more accurate, useful and natural-sounding.

For everyone, the secret is to answer in the form of real-life examples, and not to resort to merely reciting lists of favourable-sounding adjectives like 'hard-working' and 'reliable', else you might just see your interviewer's eyes roll when they hear you using the same words as everyone else they met that morning. After all, anyone can string adjectives together – it doesn't mean they're a true description of you.

Testimonials are what really count. There really is no substitute for them, so you should either turn up with a few or feature them where they can be easily found, such as your CV, your LinkedIn profile or personal website.

It should be said that interviewers will differ in the weight they attach to testimonials. Some are cynical, especially about LinkedIn testimonials, which they (perhaps rightly) see as just log-rolling between friends.

....

Who loves ya, baby?

Bring along testimonials from a wide range of stakeholders, with former clients being the most persuasive of all. A happy client is the raison d'être of every business, after all. If a client loves you, it will go a long way to changing the mind of an interviewer still sitting on the fence. Ideally, your testimonials should also tie in with your 'elevator pitch' that we mentioned earlier.

For maximum points, go through your contacts book to see if you can obtain a testimonial from an employee of a trade body or regulatory authority. A testimonial there will show that you've been thinking globally, beyond yourself and your immediate job description, and will definitely mark you out from the average candidate.

....

It's worth nothing that many interviews are conducted not just by your future boss but by your future colleagues too: you might modulate your answer depending on who's in the room. If it's just your future boss in there with you, the main thing they'll want to hear other people say about you is:

- You can do the job.
- You won't be a burden to manage.
- You're hungry for whatever it is the firm is offering.

But if potential workmates are in the interview with you, they're much more likely to want to hear accounts of you being fun, positive and fair. For them, you'll be adding to the atmosphere, not just the bottom line.

13. How do you deal with stress and failure?

The Real Question: When the pressure increases, will you turn into a monster, a useless blob of jelly or someone who sets a good example?

Top-line Tactic: *Don't pretend you live in a stress-free bubble. Instead, give concrete examples of the steps you take to handle pressure.*

Every job on the planet, from an entry-level post to a board-level position, is sometimes stressful in its own way. Given that reality, it's no surprise that this is a perennially popular interview question.

It should also come as no surprise that interviewers aren't hoping for you to claim to be immune from stress. Unless you're interviewing for the special forces or the most pressure-cooker corners of finance and sales, there's no need to come across as infallible. Rather, you only need to convince the interviewer that you won't crumble at the slightest hint of pressure.

As with all successful answers, the key to doing that is detail. A bland answer such as 'I don't do stress – it just rolls off my back' will at best be forgotten and at worst make you sound either less than forthright or slightly delusional about the realities of the workplace. Replace generalities with specific practices you've used to cope with stress, such as:

- exercise
- analysing the source of the stress
- prioritizing tasks
- delegating
- re-conceptualizing pressure as motivating
- deep breathing
- taking short breaks
- laughter/letting loose after work

Any combination of these or other techniques can work, as long as your answer convinces the interviewer that you're no stranger to stress and have figured out a constructive way to handle it.

14. How much money do you want?

The Real Question: Can we afford you? Are you value for money?

Top-line Tactic: *Avoid until as late as possible in the interview process.*

How and when to discuss salary is one of the most fraught – and most controversial – job-search questions. Many job seekers legitimately worry about either lowballing themselves or pricing themselves out of a potentially great job – or both.

Because this is such a meaty subject, it's been given its own section in Chapter 7 (p. 249), which lays out the leading schools of thought on negotiating your compensation package and walks you through the process of deciding which approach is right for your particular situation. Make sure you read it carefully (and do the recommended research) before entering the interview room. Questions along these lines are highly likely to come up, and answering them poorly can cost you a very large amount of money or even the job.

15. Show me your creativity

The Real Question: No hidden agenda here – are you creative?

Top-line Tactic: *Dig into Chapter 6, 'Curveball and Creativity Questions', for insights.*

Although you're unlikely to be asked this question in so many words, you'll almost certainly be asked one that has creativity as the underlying agenda.

This question references an earlier point about the astonishing rate of change in our world today. Specifically, many of the jobs we'll be doing ten years from now simply haven't been invented yet. No one knows what those jobs will be called, let alone what they'll entail. All we know is that someone, somewhere, will be among the first to recognize that things in their industry have changed, and here your interviewer is asking whether that person could ever be you.

Obviously, many of today's jobs (such as in graphic design) already require creativity, but that kind of creativity can be assessed in a portfolio. Here, regardless of what job you do, the interviewer is looking for evidence that a blank sheet of paper doesn't scare you – because the future has an awful lot of blank sheets of paper in store for us all.

Chapter 6 provides a complete rundown of the sort of creativity-probing questions you might run into in the interview room, as well as techniques to make sure you master a sometimes maddening – and even occasionally downright fun – section of many job interviews.

THREE

CAREER GOAL QUESTIONS

Unsurprisingly, interviewers want to hear where you think you are in your career and where you want to go next – hence you're very likely to be asked a potential showstopper like *Why do you want to work here?*

Within the broad requirement of wanting to know about your career goals, different interviewers have different reasons for asking:

- If you're a recent graduate, interviewers want to know that you expect to start at the bottom and work up, rather than start at the top and see how it goes from there.
- If you're in the middle of your career, interviewers want to know how you got there, where you want to go next and whether you have the energy and the ability to make the move up.
- If you're hoping to move sideways or planning a fresh start in a new industry, the interviewer will expect you to be clear about why you think you should be given a shot, and that you know what will be expected of you in the unfamiliar environment.

- If you're hoping for a job that's significantly bigger and more taxing than the one you have, the interviewer will want to know that you're motivated by something other than money – because money is usually not enough to keep most of us interested in a job we can't do or that we don't like, at least not for long.
- If you've had a large number of jobs recently, the interviewer will be keen to know why, and whether you're likely to flee from them too.

It all adds up to the same thing: no interviewer wants to get you on-board if deep down you'd rather be somewhere else. Wrong hires are not just time-consuming and expensive to deal with – they can also be acutely embarrassing to the hirer's reputation as a manager. Also, if you have no idea where you're going in your career, chances are you won't be in a position to inspire anyone else to travel with you – in which case you probably shouldn't be trying out for anything resembling a leadership role.

For all these reasons and more, you need to prepare a strong picture of your professional outlook, and be in a position to quickly relate it to the job specification and to the culture of the hiring company.

If the job is consistent with the career path you have envisaged for yourself, show them. If, deep down, you'd rather be somewhere else, then you should be.

16. Please describe the job you've applied for

The Real Question: We know you know, else you wouldn't be here – but how well can you sum it up?

Top-line Tactic: *Have the confidence to give them the briefest of answers.*

At interview, the difference between success and failure often comes down to knowing when to *stop* talking, and, when that time comes, actually having the confidence to stop too.

Most jobs require at least forty hours a week of activity, and there's probably something you could say about each hour. Therefore, this question truly does separate the gabblers from the strong and silent types.

When you hear this question, know that it is a test of your ability to summarize information concisely, not a test of the presence or absence of job skills. Once you go down the road of trying to list everything the job entails, you'll soon grind to halt in a great steaming cloud of words – assuming you don't bore them to death first.

Simply, you have to have the confidence to be brief, to pick only the essence of the job – which is usually either something to do with making a profit or keeping stakeholders happy – and then peppering that with maybe one or two everyday logistical tasks.

So let's say you're applying for the job of airline pilot:

My job is to fly passengers safely, on time, in comfort, at a profit to my employer.

And that, believe it or not, is a good answer in the eyes of many. Compare it to what you see when Googling the phrase 'Boeing 747 pre-flight checklist'.

If they want more, you might also wow them with:

- The exact job title.
- The reporting relationship, both up and down.
- Key performance indicators for you, your team or your product.
- One or two key challenges to be overcome in the industry.

17. How did you hear about the position?

The Real Question: How plugged in to our company are you?

Top-line Tactic: *If possible, take this opportunity to highlight your personal connection to, or passion for, the company.*

Could the interviewer simply be trying to find out which of their recruiting channels is bringing in quality candidates like you? Possibly that's part of the reason for asking this seemingly straightforward question, but there is also probably something of a hidden agenda.

As we mention in several questions throughout this book, potential employers are like potential dates – they want you to be interested in them specifically, not whoever happens to be available at the moment.

Questions about how you came across the job, therefore, are likely to be testing whether you sought out this particular firm or type of employer and feel strongly about what they do or whether you simply stumbled upon the job opening on a massive job board.

If it's at all the truth, now is the time to highlight your

personal connection to the company. Did you hear about the opening from a friend or contact? Here's the perfect way to mention that without sounding like an obnoxious namedropper. Did you locate the job through research into the industry or company because you had an interest in moving your career in their direction? Definitely tell your interviewer that.

Even if you came across the job simply by browsing through ads or via a recruitment agency, when you tell the interviewer that be sure to add a few details about why this opportunity in particular got you excited and fits your skills and abilities.

18. Why do you want to work at this company?

The Real Question: Have you been following us for a long time, or have you just read up on us?

Top-line Tactic: Show that you are familiar with the company's regular outputs, not just its 'About Us' page.

Many people can do a decent job of talking about their skills, experience and motivation, but fail to make a convincing case when talking about the target company. Recruitment experts report that candidates often focus on what the job will do for them, rather than what they will do for the company. These candidates need a simple shift in focus.

Genuine enthusiasm for the company and its business is a powerful way to get the interviewer to take an interest in you and your application, so you should treat this part of the question as an opportunity to show the interviewer that you've done your research on the company. Make sure that your research is current and relevant to the question, and shows that you've been keeping abreast of the company's development plans. Setting a news alert on a search engine for the company you're interviewing for can be a great help in the days preceding your interview.

You could choose to refer to a recent piece of news regarding the company's success, or its expansion plans, then explain how you would like to contribute during this exciting period of growth. What you say is part of the story, but most important is to let your enthusiasm shine through; it's all about showing you want to commit to that company, and it's not just a job.

Finally, if you are being interviewed by your prospective boss, focusing on your personal contribution has particular power; if you are looking forward to helping the company succeed, then you will also be making your prospective boss look good.

19. What motivates you?

The Real Question: Will this job, specifically, motivate you to do great work? Are you just in it for a pay cheque?

Top-line Tactic: *Put all that great preparation you did for this chapter to good use.*

Most of us go in to work each Monday morning, at least in part, so that come the end of the month we'll be paid, but as both you and your potential employer have probably discovered, people who are motivated solely by the money are rarely the most enthusiastic, productive or successful members of the team. The jobs you excel at will be ones that really get you buzzing – that you find you enjoy in some way and have some intrinsic motivation for. Your interviewer wants to know if this job will be one of those jobs for you.

Luckily for you, you've already done all the work to provide an excellent answer to any question asking about your motivation for changing jobs since you probed that question deeply in Chapter 1 ('So, you want a job?', p. 18). At this stage in the interview game you should have a solid idea of what you want out of your next career move, what sort of jobs and tasks energize you, and, hopefully, why this particular opening fits those requirements. Now all you have to do is explain what drives you to the interviewer, being sure to highlight why this job matches your motivations.

Because of this preparation, this question should be relatively straightforward but do keep in mind common pitfalls to avoid, such as:

- **Excessive flattery:** You may be interviewing for your dream job, but coming across as a complete fanboy (or girl) is only going to make you sound desperate. No job is perfect and no one likes a fawner. Make sure the interviewer knows you think the role is a great fit for your motivations, but don't overdo it.
- **Trivial motivations (at least in the eyes of the employer):** You may be looking for a shorter commute, but this isn't the time to mention it. Employers want you to be intrinsically motivated by the work itself, so avoid discussing other outside factors like slight pay increases, convenient hours or plain boredom at your old job.
- **The appearance of random chance:** Your CV might represent a whole lot of trial and error or be full of jobs you took simply because they were available at the time and seemed OK, but companies don't like to think of

themselves as the latest random employer you stumbled upon. They want you to want to work for them for carefully thought-out reasons, so make sure that when you're talking about your career motivations you emphasize a rational progression from job to job – a coherent career story – that this latest company fits into.

Put that all together, and what does a good answer look like? A thoughtful answer that lays out how your personal motivations and the specific characteristics of the job line up, such as:

I went into IT straight out of university, and while I enjoyed using my skills helping people in the organization solve their computer problems, what really motivated me was when I got to work on a project a couple of years later assessing which software tools to purchase and how we could customize them to meet our own needs.

I found that I really loved translating people's requirements into technical solutions. It was like working out the answer to a fun puzzle and it made my day when they told me how much easier the new software made their jobs. Plus, the challenge pushed me to keep learning, which is something else I find holds my interest at work. That's when I decided I eventually wanted to move into a role that combines IT and people skills . . .

20. Would you stay with your current employer if they offered you a pay rise?

The Real Question: Do you want the job or not? Am I being played off against your current boss?

Top-line Tactic: *There would be no dilemma: you want progress much more than you want money.*

Many hiring managers will have gone through the cycle of offering a job to someone who then gets a better counter-offer from their current employer. It's a common event and can cause a great deal of ill feeling. Often, all three parties end up shredding time, money and personal reputation – and you can easily end up with no job to go to at all. It's usually illegal to sack someone merely for seeking a new job, but it's always wise to keep your job hunt under your hat for as long as is practicable.

So, make it clear to your interviewer that you know your own mind. Tell them that you're moving for the sake of progress, not money. In truth, that is what you should be doing anyway: money is a temporary motivator at best. Interestingly, it's Reed's experience that almost every itchy-footed person who takes a counter-offer from their current employer is back on the market within six months, having wasted their time and burnt bridges. It doesn't hurt to say this out loud on the day.

That said, you'd probably get a better financial offer if the interviewer feels you're *potentially* unobtainable. The best way to do that is to draw a sharp distinction between money and progress:

I'd possibly stay at my current employer if they offered me a substantial promotion, but not just for more money. I can't see the people above me leaving any time soon, though, so I think I need to move if I'm going to progress.

I'm not sure that sort of counter-offer really works, anyway. I think someone's mindset and motivation are usually the key determinants of whether they succeed in a job or not; the money's secondary, to a large extent, so long as it's reasonable. My approach is that I want to keep learning, keep growing – do those things and the money will look after itself.

21. Would you be OK with the commute to this job?

The Real Question: Nobody likes a long commute; you know other candidates live closer than you, right?

Top-line Tactic: *If you're not prepared to move, say so. And if you genuinely don't mind the commute, say that too – and don't wait to be asked.*

For an innocent-sounding topic, this is a surprisingly rich question.

In some countries, legislation has made it illegal for an interviewer to discriminate on the basis of a candidate's post-code, so don't be surprised if even the most politically incorrect interviewer approaches this question a little gingerly.

But this question mainly concerns how long you'll stick around in the job and whether you can get to wherever the job needs you to be. Everybody knows long commutes are an expensive grind, and that the further away you live, the more likely you are to arrive late and frazzled. Indeed, a lengthy commute is one of the main reasons people quit, and your interviewer will be mindful of that. No employer will be upset to hear you live next door.

Be advised that one person's short commute is another's marathon, and you don't know which sort your interviewer is. If the topic arises, it's probably because the interviewer thinks you live too far out.

Geography can also play a part. For example, a candidate who lives in a congested city might feel that an eighty-minute commute is par for the course – but if that city-dweller were to go for a job in the country, an eighty-minute commute might well get them excluded if everybody else can be there in twenty.

In the short term, there's not much you can do about where you live and where the job is, but there are ways to counter the problem:

- If you're ready to move for the job, say so – and say it as though moving home is something you take in your stride, rather than one of the most stressful life events there is.
- If you're not prepared to move for the job, say that you'll bear the commute. If you've done it before and got used to it, be sure to say so. Be ready to show you've got the trip planned already, including your alternative route for travel delays.
- If the job involves lots of long-distance air travel and your interviewer is a veteran of that, you need to decide how world-weary you want to sound. If you're new to it, you've room to say that it's yet to burn you out. But if you're a frequent flyer yourself, for the sake of sounding sincere you might want to acknowledge that business air travel can occasionally be a tough gig, though it has its perks too.
- If you're one of those gods who can do good work on the train or on the plane, say so – because few can.

22. How does this job fit in with your career plan?

The Real Question: How much do you really want to solve my immediate problem? What about after that?

Top-line Tactic: *Interview for the job, not the employer.*

To answer this question well, it helps to have a little insight into the world of recruitment. Particularly, it helps to know that it can get on a recruiter's nerves when you apply for any old job at company X simply because you want to work at company X no matter what. It's more common than you might think – a lot of trainspotters want to get jobs on the railway, for example. They often don't make great railway employees, for obvious reasons.

Recruiters deal primarily in jobs, not careers. Yes, a recruiter is supposed to find people good enough to get promoted and give many years of service to their employer, but the recruiter's immediate and most important task is to find someone who can fill a specific vacancy. Therefore, there's not much a recruiter can do with the news that you've always wanted to work for Ferrari or Google or Amnesty International or any other outwardly attractive employer. Similarly, too many people simply say that they want to progress 'into management' without showing they know what management involves, other than more money and a bigger car.

It's understandable to think as much about your career as your next job, but there's a balance to be struck. Err too far on the side of thinking about your career and you will become the kind of candidate who is a daily nuisance to a recruiter. A recruiter's advice to you, therefore, is to interview for the job, not the company.

What follows is almost everything your employer will need to hear:

I plan to do this job well enough that you'll tell me where you want me next.

Obviously you can flesh it out by talking about your ambitions and passions, about how the role will enable you to learn and progress to the next step, but otherwise please know that this question is about testing your commitment to the employer's immediate problem.

To put it another way, and if you'll forgive an old joke:

A job hunter sees a sign in window that says 'Handyman Wanted'. He walks in:

I see you're advertising a vacancy for a handyman. I'd like to apply.

Great! Do you know how to put up shelves?

No.

Hmm – can you change a plug?

Nope.

OK, well, can you paint walls?

Nope.

So what makes you a handyman?

I live next door.

23. Give me the names of three companies you would like to work for

The Real Question: We want you here – but will you love it here? Do you understand the competitive terrain?

Top-line Tactic: *Use your research to draw distinctions between the usual suspects in your industry vs the new kids on the block.*

If you hear this question, it's a good sign. The interviewer wouldn't ask it if they weren't concerned about your hopes and dreams. Great candidates are always thin on the ground in any industry so, when one comes along, it's natural for an interviewer to start worrying that the competition will snap them up.

This question is not to be confused with *Where else have*

you applied/Who else are you interviewing with? (p. 94) – as here you're being asked to emphasize the companies you'd *choose* to work for. Or at least, that's the surface wording. In fact, the interviewer will still want to see some sign that you're hungry for whatever the interviewer is offering. Consequently, this is not a close-your-eyes-and-dream question, despite surface appearances.

All considered, we've got three suggestions you could talk about:

1. The hiring firm.
2. The hiring firm's closest rival.
3. The upstart newcomer.

It never hurts to say that you'd be prepared to work for the interviewer's closest rival (note 'prepared', not 'super-keen'). That will be evidence of a consistently applied career plan, but more importantly it will get the interviewer's adrenalin going and underscore that you're not going to be on the market for ever.

....

It's usually never a good idea to describe one company as being interchangeable with another. Most of us need to feel that their employer does things differently from the rest, so, if you're going to mention a rival firm, avoid any suggestion that they all look the same to you.

....

If you want to be bold and memorable, save the last of your three choices for a new, upstart firm operating *just* outside of your industry, or at the bleeding edge of it. Most industries are now so riven with change that there is nearly always a 'challenger' company – usually small and quirky – whose approach might well turn the established industry on its head. This will show that you're on top of competitive threats and trends. It will also ring the interviewer's bell, as they'll have likely been paying insufficient attention to the challenger company. As soon as they hear good candidates talking about working for a challenger, their adrenalin will start pumping in a wholly positive way. As far as the interviewer should think, maybe you're just the sort of person who could join that upstart firm and help them on their way.

Ultimately, the only answer that the interviewer wants to hear is: 'I'd like to work right here, right now'. Therefore, you should finish by reminding the interviewer your reason for showing up.

Like anyone who wants to work here at B—, I wouldn't mind being at M— either. But although you might both be similar on the surface, every firm always has its individual approach, and I prefer B—'s. It's the one that best suits my skills and experience.

Apart from M—, I think it would be an interesting learning experience to work for T— Motors, just to see how a start-up views the industry. Maybe they're not here to stay, but I know people there and I know the firm is daring to be different.

To answer your question, in order of preference, my three would be B—, M— and T—.

See also *What is your dream job?* (p. 98)

24. Where else have you applied? / Who else are you interviewing with?

The Real Question: Is a competitor about to snap you up?

Top-line Tactic: *Sound as though you're in demand.*

In sales there's a well-known and highly effective persuasion principle called social proof. Basically, the idea is that people want what other people want. If something is popular, it must be desirable. When you try to book a hotel room and the website you're using says 'Only two rooms remaining!' in bold red letters, it's employing social proof. They're betting that because others are choosing this hotel, you will be more likely to choose it as well.

Interviewers are just as susceptible to social proof. If other companies are thinking of hiring you that will almost certainly affect their opinion of you and your abilities. Answering this question well comes down to subtly suggesting not only that you're serious about your job search and the particular industry or niche you've chosen, but also conveying that you're a hot quantity that won't be on the market long. You don't want to brag or exaggerate, but if at all possible you do want to make sure they know you have options – though of course the option you'd prefer to take is the one they're offering.

The best way to strike this balance is often to be brief – leave them wanting more information. Simply mention a few other companies you've applied to, choosing close competitors or well-regarded firms if you can, and leave it at that. Another approach if you don't feel comfortable naming names is to stress the similarities between the roles you've applied for. This tells the interviewer that you've carefully thought out what sort of job you're after and are conducting a smart, targeted job search – the type of job search that's most likely to see you scooped up by a rival quite quickly if the company doesn't act.

25. Why have you changed jobs so frequently?

The Real Question: Will you leave this job mere months after we hire you?

Top-line Tactic: *Explain each move in terms employers can sympathize with.*

In the past, a person would often stay with a particular company for decades. This is not so common today. Thanks to economic uncertainty, redundancies and the greater instability in our early careers, times have totally changed. One recent survey found that 91 per cent of young people expect to stay in their jobs for less than three years.

But while 'job hopping' may be the new normal, that doesn't stop interviewers from being nostalgic for the good old days of long stints of service. Many continue to view frequent job changes (say less than a year for those early in their career and less than two on more than one occasion later on) with suspicion. The more you've moved around, the more they're likely to wonder whether you'll abandon ship mere months after they hire you, leaving them stuck paying the considerable costs of your recruitment without accruing much benefit. Alternatively, but just as bad for you, they could conclude that it's your shoddy work that's forced you to move on repeatedly.

Therefore, you need to take this question very seriously. What sort of answer is unlikely to reassure the interviewer? Certainly anything that makes you sound simply flaky ('I was bored'), mercenary ('Another company offered me a bit more money') or incompetent ('It was clear I wasn't going to get a promotion' or, worse, 'There just wasn't anything for me to do for some reason').

So what sorts of explanations will an interviewer usually sympathize with? There are several:

- **Short-term contract/project-oriented work:** The job was never intended to be long-term in the first place.
- **Relocation:** Obviously you couldn't keep working in city A if you needed to move to city B for personal reasons.
- **Career advancement:** If you were unable to grow or develop your skillset with one employer (perhaps due to its size or market niche) and an opportunity to learn and grow at another came up, it's understandable that you would seize the chance. Employers will appreciate your ambition.
- **Change of employer type:** Some people who work at large companies yearn to join a small firm. Others find themselves in a lone-wolf position when they want to work with a team. If you needed to make a switch to find the right working environment, explain that decision with confidence.
- **Structural changes at the company:** Did a particular client pull their business unexpectedly? Did a cost-cutting exercise result in the merging of departments or the closure of an office? Interviewers understand that these sorts of changes are beyond the control of most people and may mean you have to move on. Be warned, though, they might ask why you specifically were the one to take the fall. Hopefully you can give them a good reason that has nothing to do with the quality of your work or interpersonal skills.

However, explaining your various job moves in a way that

owns your missteps is only half the battle. Once you explain why you left those other jobs, you also need to spend a little time reassuring the interviewer why you definitely won't be leaving this one.

If you explain a lateral move by saying you had a strong desire to gain international experience, for instance, it's important to then note either that the global scale of the company you're currently interviewing for makes it a perfect place to continue in that direction, or, if that's not the case, that the travel bug is now out of your system. If you go into detail about why company X wasn't the right fit, make sure you spend some time explaining why this company most assuredly is.

Framed this way, your many jobs can be sold as a long, qualification-building quest in search of the perfect position, a position that you're thrilled to be interviewing for now.

26. What is your dream job?

The Real Question: Can we help you on your way, or is this the wrong job for you? Do you really want to work here at all?

Top-line Tactic: *Play down the dream, play up the things your dreams are made of.*

Does the interviewer really want to know your deepest and most heartfelt dream? Maybe, but probably not. For that reason, you should treat this question as a bit of fun, respond in good humour and then move on quickly. Whatever you do, do not take this question too seriously.

Our dreams tend to be unavailable to us, almost by definition, and there's not much your interviewer can do about it. Your interviewer only has one job on offer. That job was drawn up before anyone knew you and your dreams even existed.

Consequently, the following two answers are likely to be taken as insincere or misguided.

- My dream job is . . . the job we're talking about today.
  (They probably won't believe you, which means you're in trouble.)
- My dream job is . . . to be an astronaut.
  (You're in trouble if they *do* believe you.)

Uppermost on the interviewer's mind is the desire to avoid job churners. If your interviewer constantly hires people who want to work somewhere else, one way or another your interviewer will soon be heading for the exit themselves.

Here's a Reed recruiter talking about this question:

I've lost a lot of candidates on the 'dream job' question. People are too honest. They talk about dreams that are completely different from what they're interviewing for. They think it shows ambition, but hirers hate having to re-recruit.

It's OK if your employer is offering a path to your dream, and a genuine prospect of getting there, but that takes knowledge of what the interviewer is looking for. You need to articulate each step, and show that you know where you are in the sequence of those steps.

There is no such thing as a lawyer who never loses a case, or a mechanic who can keep your car going for ever, or a therapist who can solve absolutely anyone's problems. Such jobs exist only in dreams – and that's your clue to answering this question. You can get the 'dream' part out of the way by saying that you would like to *do a real-world job to a surreal, dream-like extent*. One Reed recruiter did just that when she said:

My dream job would be a fairy job-mother, giving everyone the job of their dreams with no rejections or disappointments.

This answer works because only in dreams would everyone get every job she found for her candidates, but still her answer relates to the job she was interviewing for at the time, namely a recruiter at Reed. It's exaggerated, but exaggeration is in the question itself.

Another way to go is to refer to the role by its specification, not its title.

My dream job would be one where I communicate with customers, use my expertise to solve their problems and make everyone who meets me go home happy.

Equally, you might piece together an answer using your personal aspirations. This has the effect of answering the question without saying too much.

My dream job would be one that I found totally absorbing and stimulating, where I was recognized as someone who always broke new ground in my field. It's usually not possible to tell in advance how much any job might deliver on those criteria, so mainly they're just a bit of a guiding star – a way of dealing with whatever situation the job puts me into.

We'll finish with advice for younger or inexperienced candidates: you can't really afford to dream at this stage of your career, so just focus on knuckling down and becoming good at what you do. If you say that out loud, as matter-of-factly as you just read it here in this book, you're bound to score well.

27. What's your ideal work environment?

The Real Question: Are your preferences compatible with how we do business here?

Top-line Tactic: *Say that what you want is what they're offering.*

Some companies are competitive, others more team-oriented. Some are staffed with quirky non-conformists, others with buttoned-up suits – but either way, looks can be deceiving. Being a great fit for a job isn't just a matter of skills but also of cultural fit. This question is aimed at determining the fit between how you like to work and how things get done at this company.

As always, questions that seem to be about your preferences are really about the company's needs. Your first step to answering this one well is to mentally reinterpret it into the underlying question, which is: are you compatible with the culture here? Once you understand that's what they're really asking, framing your response shouldn't be difficult.

Describe the environment you find most enjoyable, being careful to choose aspects of your ideal atmosphere that match up with the company where you hope to work, and perhaps skipping over any preferences that this particular employer isn't going to be able to meet. If you're applying for a role as an accountant that requires quite a lot of solitary number crunching, for instance, you might say:

I really enjoy a good mix of collaborative work and time to be head down and really focus on my tasks. I tend to get absorbed in my work, so once I am clear on my objectives, I like having space to really concentrate. I don't mean to sound like a hermit, though. Everyone runs into

questions once in a while, so it's great to have teammates around to
bounce ideas off and ask for pointers and better ways of working.

If you're applying for a commission-driven sales role, on
the other hand, stressing your capacity for alone time really
isn't going to win you any points. In that case, you might go
with something like:

I'm really competitive by nature so I find environments where there is a
lot of professional rivalry really help to drive me to do my best work.
Also, sales can be stressful at times, so it's good to have friendly team-
mates around I can joke with to let off steam from time to time. In
previous jobs, I've found that meeting up with colleagues socially now
and again has helped create a good team spirit at work.

28. Why do you want to leave your current job?

The Real Question: Do you know what this job is? And, to be a
little paranoid, do you have some murky problem that I can't
see now? Are you about to get fired? Help me out here.

Top-line Tactic: *It's not about you. Link your answer to what the*
company needs.

This question is rarely a showstopper – unless you want to
leave your job for a negative reason. Sadly there often *is* a
negative reason for leaving, even if it's not your fault. If that's
you, don't let this question cause panic. It is always possible
to give a sincere and positive answer regardless of your
circumstances.

First, you can never know for certain what the interviewer

is thinking, especially if you've just met for the first time. The interviewer might have assumed nothing but good things about you. Maybe they just intend the question to be an innocent warm-up, not a confession-seeker. Try to answer the question put to you rather than the question you *fear* they're asking – the latter will lead you into trouble almost inevitably.

All the same, falling out with your boss or your colleagues will often be the precise reason you're applying. After all, work is complicated. *People* are complicated. Falling out is so common that there's even a saying about it:

People don't leave companies; they leave people.

Maybe you're bored and frustrated by what you do all day. You want a change of scene, or some progress. Maybe you need more money.

The point is this: you're probably a perfectly normal human being. Wanting or needing to move on is just part of life, even if it's not always to be welcomed.

So, your starting point is to *feel in your heart that you've nothing to hide*. If you feel you're the only person in the world who can't stand their current job, you'll be on the back foot and you will find it hard to sound natural and convincing. You will start to sweat. Your interviewer might pounce on your discomfort and start asking you much harder questions.

To prevent all that, you need to focus outwards. Remember that interviews are ultimately *not about you*. They're not about your terrible boss or your measly salary, or what you want from your next job. All those things come into play but, at heart, interviews are about solving somebody else's problems, not yours.

Therefore your answer should be linked to what's on offer

and what's expected of you. Show you're running towards something, not running away.

It is at this point that good research will really pay off, for it will allow you to speak with sincerity when drawing distinctions between your current job and the vacancy. If you feel your industry is 'Coke and Pepsi', where one company is supposedly much like another, you're not researching hard enough.

The above advice boils down to one of two skeleton answers:

- In my current job I do X. You do X here too, but *this is a better place to do X*. Here's how I would do X for you.
- My employer does X, *but you do Y, and Y is what I want*. Y is also what I'm good at and enjoy. Here's how my CV relates to Y.

In both scenarios, it's possible to give a sincere and useful answer without once mentioning your terrible boss. He was never going to solve your interviewer's problems, so why bring him into the room?

You're doing a lot of biotechnology investments here. I think biotechnology is the future, and I find it huge fun too. I do like what I'm doing now; but it's not quite biotechnology, although it's closely related. On a personal note, I've always thought it best to change roles before reaching a plateau. Switch while I'm still on the way up, you know? I've decided now feels the right time for a move.

29. Talk me through (the gaps in) your CV/ career history

The Real Question: Did you stay at home watching TV for six months? Were you in jail? Is there something wrong with your mindset?

Top-line Tactic: *The best defence is offence – use your time productively when you're out of work. If you have a gap, be prepared to explain it.*

The studies on how employers view the long-term unemployed make for grisly reading. One recent bit of research, out of Northeastern University in the USA using fictitious CVs, found managers would rather hire someone with *no* relevant experience than someone who has been out of work for longer than six months. This is only one study among many that reached the same conclusion.

Given the recent economic troubles, it is hugely unjust that some firms see people who have been long-term unemployed as potentially lazy, embittered or out of date, but some do. It's not fair, but there it is. So when an interviewer is probing long gaps in your work history, they're really trying to find out whether you've a flaw in your work ethic or your mindset.

The only way to counter these worries is to prepare for the question. If you have a gap, it *will* come up. Many people have perfectly acceptable reasons for gaps in their employment record such as:

• Taking time out to raise children.
• Caring for an ill family member.

- A medical issue or accident.
- Education or further training.
- Travelling.

If any of these apply to you, good. Simply tell the interviewer what you were up to in a non-defensive manner and stress how ready you are to get back to work. Emotional matters should be dealt with matter-of-factly but not dwelled on. Turn the conversation back to your enthusiasm for returning to work as quickly as possible without sounding uncaring about a major illness or loss.

Further training is the most likely reason to be viewed favourably. Also, if you were on a gap year or other adventure abroad, many interviewers will see that as a sign of your gumption, adaptability and curiosity (especially if you're young), but you should take care to emphasize that the travel bug is now thoroughly out of your system and you're ready to settle down.

Again it's unfair, but medical issues can be viewed with wariness if the employer thinks you're likely to fall ill again or take a lot of sick leave. If true, stress that the problem is resolved and won't affect your future performance.

If you have been out of the labour market for years owing to family commitments, it generally pays to emphasize that you kept yourself up to date with events in your industry and that your skills remain sharp. Did you work occasionally as a consultant or on a contract basis? Include that on your CV and in your response. Did you apply your skills in a voluntary context, such as putting your marketing acumen to use chairing the charity drive at your children's school? That's a good thing to tell the interviewer. If you had a chance to learn anything relevant, from social media to a foreign language, by all means mention that.

What if none of the above applies to you and you were simply unable to get a job?

First, in the current economy, you're not at all alone. This situation can be hugely anxiety-inducing for a job seeker, but handled well the bias against people who have been unemployed can be countered. Accomplishing this, however, involves taking action long before any interview.

If you're out of work now, don't sit around doing nothing! Volunteer, take a class, attend seminars and conferences in your industry, teach yourself a technical skill, take on small projects as a freelancer, or otherwise get out there and prove you're determined to be productive and engaged. That way, when you're asked to walk the interviewer through the gaps in your CV, you can be honest and say that, while it took a while to find the right position after you left ABC Ltd, you used your time doing X, Y and Z, learning valuable lessons for the job at hand all the while. Interviewers understand that life is complicated and difficulties crop up. They just want to be reassured that you've met those difficulties head on rather than giving in to pessimism or inertia.

We should also add a word of advice for people who've spent time at Her Majesty's Pleasure. A 2010 study by the National Policing Improvement Agency estimated that some 9.2 million people in the UK have a criminal record.* That's one in seven of us.

Some firms take a commendably progressive view of prison leavers, most notably the national shoe-repair business Timpson. It is said that Timpson employs more ex-offenders than

---

* Approximately 900 of them were serving police officers, according to various Freedom of Information requests published in 2012 – which goes to show that a person with a criminal record shouldn't consider rejection at interview to be a foregone conclusion.

any other business in the UK; the firm opens training workshops in jail and sixteen of their high-street shops are managed by ex-prisoners. There should be more firms like Timpson, firms that combine profitability with a willingness to offer a second chance in life, but sadly there aren't enough of them. UK law recognizes this and tries to strike a balance between individual interests and the firm's interest. The law says that there is no obligation for a candidate to disclose criminal convictions for spent sentences – and in many cases it is actually illegal for an employer to refuse employment to an individual because of a previous crime.

So the law gives ex-offenders a degree of protection, and in return ex-offenders should tell interviewers the truth about their past. It won't be easy. Nevertheless, talk up your skills and highlight any positive changes in your mindset, your personal circumstances or your peer group since you were convicted.

FOUR

CHARACTER QUESTIONS

We don't have much space in this book for the input of ancient Greek philosophers – except for Heraclitus, whose writing is so brief that there's room for it in any book. Heraclitus' most famous phrase is just three words long, yet it manages to describe all of human history:

'Character is destiny'

Was there ever a more succinct performance review than that?

Our character is the single most reliable predictor of what we achieve and where we end up, both in the workplace and in life in general. That's why every good interviewer will want to put your character at the centre of the conversation.

And so they should. Read a biography of any highly successful person, be they an entrepreneur, scientist, actor or anyone else at the top of their game and it'll be clear that their character counted towards their success much more than a high IQ, good looks, money, a fancy education or good connections. All those other things help, but character can trump them all. Some people like to say that their career makes them who they are, but I think it's the other way round – a person's career emerges out of their character.

Don't believe me? Here are three people who were supposedly blessed with everything in life that one might need to succeed and stay on top, yet they were all led by their character into failure or disgrace:

- **Good looks and money:** If you've seen Martin Scorsese's *The Aviator*, you'll know that the real-life Howard Hughes was a rich, outgoing and devilishly handsome entrepreneur with a string of Hollywood actress girlfriends. He was still rich and handsome the day he bumped his head in a plane crash, causing his character to change for the worse. Although fully functional, he became progressively paranoid and withdrawn to the point where eventually he died a lonely recluse, when I daresay no billionaire has to. As Heraclitus could have predicted, Hughes's destiny changed the day his character changed.
- **Good education and connections:** The blue-blooded Jonathan Aitken went to Eton, then to Oxford and then on to the Cabinet – and then to jail, for committing perjury during a 1997 trial. He could have avoided jail if he'd told the truth in court, but that would have meant a loss of face, and for Aitken's character that would have been too much. To his credit, Aitken used his time in jail to face up to himself, becoming an articulate advocate for the welfare of his fellow prisoners. Nevertheless, it was his character that put him in jail in the first place.
- **High IQ:** Some readers will remember Clive Sinclair, the British inventor and copper-bottomed genius who brought us the revolutionary Sinclair Spectrum computer. He's someone with a larger IQ than most, but he's also an endearingly geeky character who believed that everyone

would want the same thing *he* wanted, namely to drive around in one of his Sinclair C5s. For those who don't remember, a C5 looked like a coffin crossed with a golf cart. Doubtless its engineering was brilliant – but nobody wanted to drive a coffin-shaped golf cart and, for all his genius, Sinclair never saw that coming. I certainly don't mean to suggest that Sinclair was a morally bad character. It's just that some people can't see beyond their own tastes and won't be told any different; when those people occupy leadership positions, commercial disaster often ensues.

Ultimately all the technology, disciplinary proceedings and legal regulations in the world cannot protect against someone who lacks integrity or self-knowledge.

Most interviewers think that way too, so you can expect plenty of questions based around your character, in particular your integrity. These questions often come in the form of moral dilemmas, such as *Tell me about a time when your supervisor asked you to do something you knew to be morally wrong*. It's a dilemma because you either disobeyed your boss or you did something dubious. But presumably you opted to do one or the other – perhaps by doing what you were told, or by standing up to your supervisor. Either way, your true north is revealed. Very often your chosen course of action to resolve the dilemma is less important to the interviewer than showing that you knew what you were doing and why.

The best way to tackle a character question is to show that you make conscious and clear decisions according to a set of values that you'll bring with you to the new company, and that you can live with the consequences of your values.

There are certain things that a CV can reveal – your degree, your career path and your major achievements, for example. For others, a CV is less than useless. Insight into your character definitely falls into the latter category, and is something that an interviewer *needs to know about*. The questions you'll find in this section have been specifically designed to uncover the essence of you.

30. How was your journey here?

The Real Question: Ready to begin the interview? Five . . . four . . . three . . . two . . .

Top-line Tactic: *A big smile and a short answer that's long on gratitude.*

You might think this isn't a character question, but you'd be surprised at the number of nuances and possibilities within it. First impressions count.

Almost every interviewer has a warm-up question. They may vary in tone and wording but they all mean pretty much the same thing:

Hi! Isn't this odd? I'm almost as nervous as you are. Anyway, let's begin the interview. Good luck to us all.

'How was your journey?' is a good warm-up question simply because every candidate has a journey and, if it was a good journey, it's possible to answer in only a few words without causing offence. (It's also a blessing of a question if you live nearby – let the interviewer know with a 'Yup, just twenty minutes on a direct train from where I live.' As mentioned elsewhere, they won't be sad if you live next door.)

It might seem weird that anyone would need help answering a warm-up question, since both the Q and the A are mostly content-free. Nevertheless there are three perfectly good reasons for going over warm-up questions here:

First, when you're nervous, it's easy to misinterpret a warm-up question for an interview that has begun in earnest, causing you to think that there is a hidden meaning to an innocuous question. For example, it's not unknown for a candidate to misinterpret 'How did you find the journey?' as meaning 'How come you're late?', prompting an undignified bout of unnecessary apologies. Nor is it unknown for a nervous candidate to blurt a smart-alec response when a simple 'Fine, thanks' would have done.

Nine times out of ten, the warm-up question is merely everyone clearing their throat, so there's no need to zing them with *what* you say, only *how* you say it. The warm-up question is your first chance to deliver a smile and a happy, confident tone of voice.

When interviewing for jobs at Metro Bank UK, the US banking billionaire Vernon Hill looks for someone to smile in the first thirty seconds. No smile by the half-minute mark, no job with Vernon. As he puts it: 'It is harder to teach someone to smile than it is to teach them banking skills.'

Second, if you're an old hand at interviewing and keen to get down to the real interview talk, you might see the warm-up question as something to wave out of the way – and that could show up as a half-hearted response.

Instead, you should aim to come across as though the warm-up question is a kind inquiry into your wellbeing. In truth, *it is* an inquiry into your wellbeing, only it's in respect of possible interview nerves, not your journey there.

Third, it's likely that someone, somewhere, helped you to find the interview room, so offer your thanks to them even if they're not in the room with you. Their help might have taken many forms, whether it's the 'How To Find Us' standard info pack from the HR department or a friendly greeting and direction from the receptionist. In whatever form the help arrived, acknowledge it – preferably with names. Most people don't bother remembering that Tom in HR sent some useful directions, and that's exactly why you should mention him. It's what a person of good character would do.

31. Where does your boss think you are now?

The Real Question: How easily tempted are you to lie?

Top-line Tactic: Simple – don't lie.

Some readers might think this question belongs in the 'Curve-ball' chapter, because it certainly does feel like a curveball when it gets thrown at you. However, it's best thought of as a character question, as deep down it's really just a simple inquiry into how open and honest you are. Simple, but potentially devastating.

Some would say that job hunting calls for a 'white lie', where you tell your boss that you need time away to take care of a 'personal matter' when really you're interviewing for a job. But a white lie is a self-serving concept. We can all think of people we might lie to, but few we would like to have lie to us. It's wrong to hope that everyone will tell you the truth even while you're prepared to finesse others. In any case, 'personal matter' is poor communication. It could mean anything from bereavement to ill health, neither of which should be invoked lightly. If you cite personal matters as the reason for your absence, and then get found out, you'll have made things much worse by having played on your boss's heartstrings.

But it's still a thorny issue. If you lie to your boss about where you are, the interviewer won't think much of you, but if you tell your boss the truth he'll probably never look at you in the same way again.

The only logical courses of action are either to book a day's holiday for your interview or, if you have the negotiating power, to ask that you be interviewed outside office hours (i.e. breakfast, lunch or evening). If you ask for an out-of-hours interview and point out that you're not prepared to lie to your current boss, your prospective employer ought to give you brownie points. If they don't, you've learned something about them that's truly worth knowing.

One possible exception is when a firm announces impending redundancies. Then, it's *probably* OK to say that you're interviewing elsewhere. Once a company makes it clear that you and it no longer have a future together, few bosses would be mean enough to scupper your escape plans.

32. What are your core values?

The Real Question: Do your values line up with ours?

Top-line Tactic: *Make sure you know the company's values as well as your own.*

Companies, like people, have values, and if an interviewer is asking about yours, chances are it's to find out whether their organizational values match up with your personal ones. To impress, it helps to know what the organization's values actually are. That's why it's important to look around their website before the interview and get a sense of what type of company you're dealing with – mission driven and sustainability conscious? Cut-throat and competitive? Obsessed with safety or more interested in innovation?

Hopefully, the company's core values were part of what prompted you to apply to them in the first place, so there's probably significant line up between your principles and theirs. Highlight the points of overlap when you're asked this question.

If you do that, you're halfway to a good answer. To get across the finish line you're going to need to provide evidence. Don't just tell them you value 'honesty'. Also offer them an anecdote or story that illustrates you actually live by that value. Vague statements about being a hard worker or big believer in fairness will go in one ear and out the other. If you include a story about that time you helped out by working all weekend, drove a hundred miles out of your way to deliver a document, or volunteered for an unpleasant duty, you'll make your claims memorable.

33. What are your hobbies and interests?

The Real Question: Do you pass the airport test?

Top-line Tactic: *Share a genuine passion, but don't make it sound like it's more important than your work.*

Have you heard of the airport test? In the world of recruiting, the airport test is a quick gut check to determine whether a candidate is going to fit in with your company culture and be pleasant to work with. It's quite straightforward: interviewers simply ask themselves how they would feel if they had to pass a few hours waiting for a delayed plane with you.

Your ability to entertain while sharing a snack in the departure lounge may not sound like a core job skill, but some of the world's best companies, from top investment banks to Google, admit to using the airport test when hiring, so keep it in mind when answering this question.

Your exact answer doesn't usually matter, but it is important you communicate two key factors alongside whatever you choose to reveal. The first is authenticity. Don't ever say you love doing X when it's something you barely ever do. No one wants to pass the time in an airport with a fantasist. Only offer a subject you can converse about in some detail and with enthusiasm: your interviewer may be a fellow enthusiast and ask follow-up questions.

Second, you want to convey that you are a rounded, engaging person with interests outside the office without giving the impression that your after-hours passions, whatever they are, will impinge on your commitment to the job. Strike the right balance here by mentioning *something*, but don't plant any seeds of doubt about your commitment to work in the interviewer's mind. For instance, your passion for music is likely to make you seem interesting and human, but if you gush about moonlighting as a nightclub DJ, the interviewer might rightly start to wonder how your late-night shenanigans will gel with the 8 a.m. start time the job you're applying for demands.

34. Tell me about your first job

The Real Question: How's your work ethic?

Top-line Tactic: *Whatever you thought of your first job, now's the time to recount any positive lessons it taught you.*

Many interviewers believe that your attitude to your first job says a lot about your attitude to work in general, that if you were too indulged to do menial work in your schooldays then maybe you're still a snob now. It's not a particularly scientific theory but it is a popular one, so you should come to interview prepared to talk about your days waiting on tables, mucking out stables and delivering newspapers.

Recent graduates routinely get this all wrong. They'll play down the menial jobs in their CV, in favour of talking about their dissertations, choice of university or so much other stuff that means the world to younger people but often means little to a grizzled interviewer.

But for the same reason, it is very easy for a recent graduate to set themselves apart from the pack on this subject. All they need do is *appear delighted to be asked about their first job*. That's guaranteed to leave a mark on your interviewer, as most recent grads dismiss the topic with a few brief put-downs. Nor will it hurt the recent graduate to mention what else was going on in their life while they were working – notably exams.

My first ever job was as a stock assistant in a supermarket. That taught me lots of things that I'd never have learned in school, such as dealing with the public and how to juggle things with a profit in mind.

Then a vacancy arose on the checkouts and I applied for it and got it. I enjoyed that more because there was a lot more customer interaction and it made a nice break from all the GCSE revision I was doing at the time. I think it might even have helped because my results were better than some of my friends who gave up their part-time jobs to study full time.

I think a first job instils a good work ethic for young people – that if you want something, you have to work for it.

The important thing here is to tie in the concepts of a first job setting the tone for a good work ethic and an ability to multitask.

Sadly, starter jobs for early teens, such as a paper round, seem to be on the wane. If you've never had such a job, you are at a distinct disadvantage. It is therefore vital you make it clear that you still have a lot to learn, but that you can't wait to roll up your sleeves and get stuck in. This, for a recent graduate, will be more impressive than pointing out all the proxies for your abilities, such as your degree, your dissertation, your university, what you're reading or what your mother or father does for a living. None of those things matter much to your employer.

And if you're one of the few people whose first job became a career, it might be overegging it to say that you knew from an early age that that line of work was what you wanted to do with your life, but you could legitimately say it's kept you happy all this time.

The bottom line: there's no such thing as a bad first job. They're all useful.

35. Who do you admire and why?

The Real Question: What are your fundamental values?

Top-line Tactic: The why is more important than the who – make sure you show you value something the company values too.

When an interviewer asks about role models, what they really want to know is what qualities you value in other people, but also in yourself. For this reason, the 'why' half of this question counts a lot more than the 'who'. Select someone who will highlight personal qualities that you admire, but which are also likely to prove valuable in the particular role you are applying for.

Going for a management position? Then select a great leader. Applying for an entry-level role that might give you a shot at working your way to the top? Then make it clear you're willing to learn. If you're a nurse, perhaps focus on empathy and service.

Whether you choose someone everyone knows, an obscure historical figure, or someone you know personally, it's more about the spin you give your answer than anything else.

If you choose someone widely admired, such as Nelson Mandela, your answer is unlikely to stick in the interviewer's mind or sound terribly personal or convincing. It probably won't kill your chances of getting the job, but it won't advance them much either.

Name a second-century Persian military leader that an Oxford don would have to look up and you run the risk of coming across as trying far too hard – unless, of course, you can back up your choice with a truly compelling story. Anyone controversial can also present pitfalls. If you choose a modern politician, for instance, be aware that you might be thought of as revealing your political affiliation, an affiliation the interviewer might not share.

Many people admire their parents or other close family and friends. It's perfectly acceptable – perhaps even charming – to choose your mum, but again, make sure you explain why she's a personal hero to you in a way that maps onto the requirements of the job, such as:

I would say my mum because she's brought up four children on her own, running her own B&B. She was a great example of determination in the face of hardship and the value of hard work to me.

Be warned that mothers and fathers are a very popular choice of answer here – don't pick them unless you have a very well-thought-through answer, else you risk making the interviewer's eyes glaze over.

36. If you could bring anyone to this company from where you currently work, who would it be?

The Real Question: Who do you need around you in order to function well? What does this company need to function well? What are our competitors doing that maybe we aren't?

Top-line Tactic: Chose someone who would help you do the job, not someone who would help you get through a boring day.

This question sheds light on a number of your key motivations, including what you want from the people around you and how seriously you take your career.

Some co-workers are huge fun, but that's no reason to bring them with you. Be prepared to give a wholly productive and professional reason for your choice.

It's best to say you'd bring someone who stands to add something to the hiring company, or someone who would add to *you*. You should reflect on your ability to connect and to recognize a quality in someone that helps you to achieve more yourself.

This question is also a free pass to show you know the hot topics in your industry.

Start with a name, then identify the hot topic, then the reason for your choice.

I'd bring Tom, our legal compliance officer. Five years ago the banking industry was comparatively unregulated, but now it seems like we have to deal with new legal restrictions every day. Suddenly, it's often only the compliance officer who can say whether a new product might even be legal, let alone any good. What I like about Tom is that he goes further than most compliance officers. He doesn't just stop things from going wrong; he helps me create stuff as well. I think most banks see compliance as a cost, but a good compliance officer is a competitive advantage, and Tom's a good one. He seems like a nice guy, too, although I don't really know him all that well, but he's certainly good at what he does, which is the main thing.

In choosing who you would bring with you, you're also identifying who you *wouldn't* bring. An experienced interviewer might follow up and ask about the people who didn't make your list (*You wouldn't bring your current boss? Why not?*), in which case see p. 102, *Why do you want to leave your current job?*

37. Tell me about a time you dealt with a difficult person

The Real Question: You know that everyone's difficult sometimes, right?

Top-line Tactic: *Show that you can work with anyone, even if nobody's perfect – including you.*

We've all overheard two people complaining to each other about somebody giving them a hard time at work. Your interviewer will have heard similar conversations too – because difficult people are an inevitable part of life. At a job interview, inevitability is your friend; it's a chance to talk like a real person.

Don't be tempted to say you've never worked with a

difficult person. That's a clichéd tactic – one that might be interpreted as an attempt to lie. Nor will you do yourself any favours by pleading a short work history: you might just be asked about school or university instead.

It's better to give a specific example. You could start with: *I could pretend I get on with everyone, but that wouldn't be honest . . .* That says you're a straight talker. Having roused their interest, you should then emphasize that some people are employed because they're good at what they do, not because they're easy-going.

As part of your pre-interview preparation, put some time into consciously choosing your difficult-person episode. If you don't, you could well reach for the person most easily recalled by you in the heat of the moment. That person is typically your nemesis, the memorably annoying person who brought out the worst in you.

The stakes are much higher if you opt to talk about a colleague or a customer or a boss – there you could win big or lose big. So, if the interviewer isn't specifying one of those three, see if you can recall an encounter with someone whose job it is to give you grief. You might think few such people exist, but actually the list is quite long. Some examples: someone from a rival firm, an agent for the client, a certified inspector, a journalist, a pressure group or someone from local government – they're all supposed to give you a hard time, to a greater or lesser degree.

Here's what your answer should cover:

- Could you have changed the situation?
- Did you do anything to make it worse?
- Did you listen to the other person?
- Could you have reasonably been expected to put up with it – and if not, how did you stand your ground?

- Did you keep your cool?
- Do you see the world as adversarial or consensual?

It's true that some people are just plain difficult, but that's one truth that doesn't *have* to come out of your mouth. You've more to gain by acknowledging that it takes two people to have a personality clash – that's a good note to strike before handing back.

38. When were you last angry – and why?

The Real Question: Are you a hothead? Can you handle stress?

Top-line Tactic: *Provide an example when you constructively worked through a stressful or annoying situation.*

'Angry' is a strong word. It connotes losing control, emotionally driven thinking and impulses that are destructive rather than constructive. None of these things is exactly valued in business. So while the interviewer is asking you for an anecdote about when you were angry, on the face of it you shouldn't provide one.

On the other hand, we're only human and no one gets through a working week without some degree of frustration, annoyance and stress. Claiming you have the patience of a Zen priest is certainly going to appear disingenuous. Instead, massage the question slightly to replace 'angry' with 'stressed' or 'frustrated' and offer the interviewer a time you ran into an annoying situation but were able to keep your cool and handle it constructively.

As always in interviews, beware of citing your supervisor as a source of stress. Interviewers generally take the perspective of management, so anything bad you say about your boss will probably strike them as a taste of things to come, i.e. an unreasonably disgruntled individual who can't get along with his manager. Luckily for us, the world offers plenty of other sources of annoyance. Choose one of them and say something along the lines of:

I wouldn't say I ever get really angry at work. I try to keep my emotions in check as I find it doesn't improve the situation when you get emotional. I do get stressed and annoyed from time to time, of course. For instance, once we were designing a very important project that required approval from the engineers before we could proceed. We gave them plenty of time, but when I called to check in the day before the deadline, they hadn't even looked at it. I was quite stressed about completing the project on time, so I was livid.

Shouting down the phone wasn't going to help the situation, though, so I counted to ten and asked what was the problem. Apparently, they were swamped with a project themselves and hadn't appreciated how urgent ours was. The guy I was speaking to agreed to work late to help us out. It was still tight, but we made the deadline and in the end the whole misunderstanding actually improved things because we came up with a new system to prioritize tasks so the same thing wouldn't happen again.

39. Tell me about something funny that has happened to you at work

The Real Question: Can I stand to be cooped up in the same office with you forty-odd hours a week?

Top-line Tactic: *Make a joke at your own expense.*

Humour can be a serious business. Studies (by actual business-school professors, not comedians) have shown laughter has a powerful ability to fight stress and bond teams. If your interviewer asks this question, he or she is probably looking ahead to the time when you might be working alongside each other for most of the week and wondering if you'll add to or subtract from the office laughter quotient.

The problem is while laughter is powerful stuff it's also quite personal. A joke that will have one person rolling on the floor will result in eye rolls from someone else. So while you really don't want to come across as a humourless killjoy here by drawing a blank, you also don't want to inadvertently baffle or offend your potential new employer with the episode you choose.

If you're naturally hilarious, there's probably little a book on interviewing technique can add. Just be yourself. But if you're less sure of your comedic abilities, the safest way to proceed is to skip barbed humour, mockery or the politically incorrect and simply make fun of yourself instead. It's a rare person who doesn't appreciate self-deprecation in others, so nearly all interviewers will take a joke at your own expense as a sign that you will able to help your team through tough times with your sense of humour.

Remember that time the sole of your shoe disintegrated and your teammate followed the trail to your desk, much to your embarrassment? Or that colleague's birthday party where you accidentally dropped the cake? Now is the time to break out that sort of innocuous, victimless story.

40. What is it about this job that you would least look forward to?

The Real Question: Are you going to like this job? Are you drawn to it for the right reasons? Do you have the guts for it? Is this job consistent with your career goals – and if not, what's the real reason you're applying?

Top-line Tactic: *Acknowledge an unfortunate (but key) aspect of the job and say how you have dealt with it before.*

This question is not an opportunity to pretend that the job holds zero downside for you. It is a wonderful opportunity to show you're tougher than the rest.

The clichéd answer to this question sees you cherry-pick an infrequent task and hide behind the fact that you won't be performing it very often. If you can do that *and sound like you mean it*, then good luck. In truth, most of the time you will probably come over like you're dodging the question.

A better tactic is to pick on a part of the job that nobody in their right mind would enjoy. There is not a job in the world that doesn't have obvious drawbacks. You should talk about a vacancy's difficulties in a way that proves you can handle them, preferably with reference to experience.

I think every job involves difficult choices. Sometimes you have to disappoint people, and no one in their right mind likes doing that. But I know it's not something I can avoid.

As an estate agent, I don't enjoy telling someone their house will never sell for what they're asking. There's a lot of wishful thinking in property – it's human nature. But if I don't tell them the truth, no one can move on.

I always say that the facts are friendly. It means I sometimes need to let people get angry, let off steam right in front of me – but that isn't going to kill me. I know they're usually annoyed with the situation, not me personally.

So, to answer your question, I don't look forward to disappointing people within the first two minutes of meeting them, but I do it all the time and it's not a problem.

Your interviewer will warm to you if you can gracefully acknowledge that no job gives you a buzz 100 per cent of the time, but that *this* job would enable you to feel a buzz most of the time – and that you will gladly accept that trade-off.

Final pointer: it is natural to be apprehensive about a task you've never done before, but it would be a mistake to select that task in your answer here. Without experience, you're less able to judge whether a new task is a key part of the job – plus you're forgoing a free chance to cite the relevant experience you *do* have.

Remember: you're tougher than the rest.

41. Tell me something about yourself that isn't on your CV

The Real Question: Are you going to give me a mature response? Are you a well-rounded person outside of work? And oh, I'm tired – will you take over for a bit?

Top-line Tactic: *If it advances the action, say whatever you want to say. Avoid trivia and flippancy.*

Interviews are tiring. Sometimes the interviewer needs to put their feet up, recuperate and watch you do all the hard work. This question allows them to do that.

Your answer is a test of judgement, for you'll need to reference something interesting and impressive that somehow wasn't worth putting on your CV. It also requires you to judge whether the interviewer wants to hear more about you as a person or as a professional. That's two conundrums to deal with. In the heat of the moment, a candidate who is unprepared or just inexperienced will often solve those conundrums by saying something twee, funny or pseudo-embarrassing, such as 'I am the world's biggest *Game of Thrones* fan'. It's very common for nervous candidates to reach for trivia, having assumed that everything worth saying has already been said on their CV.

So if you don't want to be the person who talks about their DVD collection at interview, remind yourself that you're there to show you can do a job. Emphasize the professional more than personal. If they want personal, show them your values and your mindset.

It is always appropriate to show that you have outside interests that are sociable and achievement-oriented, ones that involve teamwork or personal initiative.

Professional

- Did you omit to mention your first ever job? A lot of people do, but it's a mistake – all work experience counts. If your first job set you on your current career path, mention it now (see *Tell me about your first job*, p. 117).
- A project or professional episode that was far less easy than it appears on your CV – but which you conquered anyway.

Personal

- Voluntary work.
- Specific and interesting instances of your hobby – e.g. 'I ran a marathon dressed as a rhino for the Save the Rhino foundation.'
- Any groups to which you belong and regularly contribute, e.g. 'I've been involved in PADI, the Professional Association of Diving Instructors, for many years and am now a Master Scuba Diver.'

Be ready to say why you took up these activities, and how they've affected you. Ideally, you'll be able to say how your experience in them feeds directly into the job.

Being asked this question is a sign that you're doing well, so you can afford to take a little liberty. Here's a couple of answers that combine the personal AND the professional.

Well, one thing I left off my CV was that I am a demon buyer and seller of vintage clothing on eBay. I do it partly for social reasons – friends bring stuff to me that they'd probably have thrown out otherwise, and my reputation will get them the best price. I think they treat it as more of an excuse to get together, which is great, but it's also fun for me to spot value in what they think is junk, and then we all go out for a meal on the proceeds.

Well, I've mentioned company X on my CV already, but what I left off is that X was going broke when I joined it. I joined just as the economy tanked. The company employed ten people then, then headcount went down to seven, then five, then there were just two of us – the founder and me. I stuck with it, he stuck with me – and we built it back up to twenty people. I didn't have room for all that on my CV, but I think I learned more in those two years than in any other job.

42. What do you most dislike about yourself?

The Real Question: If I rattle your cage, what will you reveal about yourself?

Top-line Tactic: *Don't mistake the interview room for your psychologist's office. Reframe and answer in a professional manner.*

This one is the evil twin of the more common *What are your greatest weaknesses?* question (p. 56). While it covers similar ground, it's broader, more personal and potentially more negative. Weaknesses can be remedied. A character flaw is harder to fix.

So why would an interviewer go for this more confrontational wording? It could be with the intention of leading you into revealing deeper and more meaningful flaws, given that most candidates are well prepared for the standard weakness question. Or they might simply be trying to ruffle your feathers to see what happens when someone pushes your buttons.

Whatever the interviewer's aims, yours are clear. Don't answer the question as asked. This is an interview, not a session with your shrink, so you can leave the deepest recesses of your soul happily unplumbed. But you do have to keep your cool and answer or risk coming across as unable to handle pressure or less than self-aware. Just mentally reframe the question and respond much as you would to any other query of areas in need of improvement. Humanize yourself with a forgivable flaw that doesn't in any way preclude you from doing well at the job at hand:

Before I answer, I want to say that I don't think there's anything that I actively dislike about myself. Having said that, there are one or two character traits that I pride myself on more than others.

From quite a selfish point of view, if I had to pick something I'd like to improve, I suppose it would be how comfortable I am with delivering bad news at work. I guess I'm the same as most people in that sense – and I'm not sure it's something that's going to become easier as I gain experience.

I would prefer people to like me and I don't relish confrontation – and that's not always a useful trait to have, even if it makes the world go round most of the time.

It's never been a significant problem for me at work – touch wood – but there have been times when I haven't enjoyed parts of my job, such as when I've had to fire people or give a really bad appraisal. It would be a lot easier for me if I had a heart of ice, but that's not who I am and, most of the time, I'm glad about it.

Or, as a recent graduate, you might say:

As I'm sure you can imagine, having just come out of university there are a couple of things I wish I'd done differently recently. I'm sure my 2:1 will weigh on my mind for a while – perhaps I'd like myself a bit more if I'd put in the extra 2 per cent I needed for a First. I know my mum certainly would, anyway!

One thing that used to trouble me was how most of my housemates had a very clearly defined career path planned out in their heads, all the way up to which position they wanted to hold at a particular company by the time they reached their forties. I've never been like that, and I used to dislike the fact that I didn't have much to add to those conversations.

But I've since realized that being a bit more open-minded has its benefits, too. Take this job, for example. I may not know exactly where I want to be in twenty years, but I do know that your company's various learning and development opportunities and flexible progression options are ideal for someone like me. I have no idea what stories I'll have for my housemates at future reunions, but I'm perfectly comfortable with that.

43. How would you react if I told you that you are not the strongest candidate we have interviewed so far?

The Real Question: Show me you can fight your corner.

Top-line Tactic: Ask the interviewer why you might not measure up and try to reassure them about any concerns.

There are two possible reasons the interviewer is asking you this admittedly pretty nasty question. One, you've nearly arrived at the end of the interview and they genuinely have some reservations about your candidacy, or two, they want to see how you react when directly challenged or asked to pitch yourself.

Either way you'll benefit from keeping your cool and asking for a bit more information. If it's the first situation, the interviewer's answer will help you better counter any reservations. If it's the second, it shows you take a constructive approach to criticism and conflict. So ask something like:

I suppose I'd start by asking why you felt I wasn't the strongest candidate. Ask for some additional information about your concerns. That way I'd be better prepared to respond.

Hopefully, the interviewer will explain their doubts regarding your candidacy, if any, at which point you should use their response to tailor the next part of your answer. If a long pause hangs in the air or this turns out to be simply a hypo-thetical question, you'll have to aim your pitch as best you can without additional guidance. Either way, you should now reassure the interviewer by succinctly summing up your key selling points for this specific role.

Sometimes you'll have a gut sense of what might be giving the interviewer pause – if you lack a certain qualification or type of experience, say. In that case, you should address those concerns straight on. There's no advantage to ignoring the elephant in the room. If not, just take your best guess at what the interviewer is hoping to hear or simply decide which of your selling points bears repeating. For instance:

I know I don't have a great deal of sector-specific experience, but it could be that the division's sales figures will benefit from fresh ideas put forward by someone not entirely familiar with that corner of the indus-try. And, of course, I do have deep knowledge of other sectors, so I can see the overall picture more clearly than someone very specialized. If things are a bit stale, I think I'm the ideal person to freshen them up, even though it might take me a week or two to find my feet.

44. Is it acceptable to lie in business?

The Real Question: What are your core values?

Top-line Tactic: Show that you leave lying to people who are content to win that way.

The world is unfair. Proof? Almost everybody lies, yet nobody wants to hire a liar.

Regardless, if your interviewer gets onto the topic of lying, you should play it 100 per cent straight and say that lying is always unacceptable, and that you have moral and practical reasons for saying so.

Those reasons are writ large in the work of the Dutch management academic Fons Trompenaars. In his book *Did the Pedestrian Die?* Trompenaars poses a hypothetical moral dilemma:

Imagine you're a passenger in a car driven by your best friend. Your friend is breaking the speed limit, driving at 35 mph in a 20 mph zone. Suddenly, a pedestrian steps out. The car hits him. The police arrive. The matter goes to court. There are no witnesses. Your friend's lawyer says that if you are prepared to testify under oath that he was only driving at 20 mph, it may save him from serious consequences.

Does your friend have a right to expect you to protect him?

- a: My friend has a DEFINITE right to expect me to testify to the lower figure.
- b: He has SOME right to expect me to testify to the lower figure.
- c: He has NO right to expect me to testify to the lower figure.

Trompenaars has asked this question to literally thousands of business executives around the world. His results show, among other things, that the first thing many of us do when faced with a dilemma is squirm and bargain our way out of it, usually by suggesting a set of qualifying circumstances (in his example, by asking if the pedestrian died). In a job interview, this kind of squirming and wheedling and bargaining is not a good look. Trompenaars' work shows that it is incredibly easy to tie yourself in knots once you get onto the subject of lying. Consequently, the best tactic at interview is to aspire to perfection but also to acknowledge that people are often less than perfect. It's also wise to show that you know about the business consequences of lying:

It's never OK to lie. People do, of course, usually for some short-term gain, but I don't think it's ever worth it in the long run.

It's easy to make bad choices under pressure, and some businesses are even run in such a way that people don't know they're lying – like Enron, where half their employees genuinely thought they were innocent because they were simply following company policy.

I prefer to treat people the way I want to be treated myself, and nobody wants to be lied to. Life's much simpler if you always tell the truth. And most people will forgive you for making a mistake, but they'll never forgive a lie.

There may well be a fine line between a lie and withholding the truth, but an interview is not the time to reveal you've ever needed to think about it.

Interestingly, Trompenaars' work shows big national differences in answering his traffic-accident dilemma. Leaving aside the issue of what people say they would do versus what they would actually do, the world seems to be split between countries where there is more outward support for moral rules, and countries where it's more important to stick by your friends. (One interpretation of Trompenaars' data is that you should marry a Brazilian but drive slowly in Germany.) It all goes to show that lying is highly complex. And in interview, you don't have time to tease out those nuances – you might regret you even tried.

Lying is lying, no ifs or buts.

45. If you could go back and change one thing about your career to date, what would it be?

The Real Question: Is there something bad about you that I cannot see, and if there is, can I get you to admit it? Do you carry psychological baggage that you don't need? How readily do you forgive yourself – and others?

Top-line Tactic: *Give the interviewer a little bit of grit but never use the word 'regret' in your answer. Focus on something positive and say you wished you'd done more of it. Then stop talking.*

When racing driver Lewis Hamilton crashed in one of his first Formula 1 races, an interviewer asked him if he regretted what he'd just done. Hamilton, despite being barely out of his teens, and barely out of a smouldering wreck of a car, simply smiled and answered, 'You can't get through life without making a few mistakes.'

Thus spoke a future champion, and maybe a future champion's well-paid sports psychologist too.

To save you the price of a sports psychologist, remember this: human beings make mistakes and most of us have a few regrets. That's a warm, worldly and liberating view to take of yourself and of the people around you. Get it into your interview mindset.

If you can satisfy yourself that regrets are normal, you'll be less likely to get flustered when asked about yours. You'll be less likely to use the word 'regret' in your answer. Don't steer the conversation that way. Regret is a loaded word: don't point it at yourself.

All told, I don't have too many complaints about the way things have gone. If I could change one thing, I'd have moved into the mobile phone insurance business sooner than I did. I turned out to be good at that, and I enjoy it too. But back in the nineties I was enjoying myself selling life insurance. In those days, mobile phone insurance was something nobody ever thought of. It's easy to say with hindsight that everyone was going to insure their phones, but it was a time when hardly anybody even owned one, let alone lost one. If I'd moved into it sooner then maybe I'd have been sitting here a couple of years earlier – but who knows? Missing out on that taught me to take the odd risk in life, and I'm thankful for that.

Emphasize what you're running to, not what you're running from.

If you're unlucky, the interviewer might explicitly use the word 'regret' in the question. It would be rude not to use their language in your answer. But don't panic – just say something like:

Everybody has the odd regret, but generally regrets are unproductive because most of them are based on doing whatever we thought was right at the time . . .

. . . and then go on to give exactly the same answer as before, the answer that references the job and what you're about, with zero mention of regret.

Keep it honest and positive – but short.

46. What do people assume about you that would be wrong?

The Real Question: How well do you know yourself?

Top-line Tactic: *Demonstrate self-awareness at the same time as you put the interviewer's fears to bed.*

A question along these lines is a favourite of Zappos boss Tony Hsieh, who is famous not only for selling his shoe delivery service to Amazon for a tidy sum but also for the uniquely happy work culture he created at the company. When asked for his most indispensable interview questions in a *New York Times* interview, Hsieh offered this one: 'If you had to name something, what would you say is the biggest misperception that people have of you?'

What is he trying to find out by asking that? 'I think it's a combination of how self-aware people are and how honest they are. I think if someone is self-aware, then they can always continue to grow,' he explains.

This question probes not only your personality but also your emotional intelligence. It takes a fairly sensitive understanding of both yourself and others to grasp not only how you'd like to be perceived but also where you fall short and why.

So how should you think about answering? As always, start from a position of honesty. If you portray yourself as a sensitive soul under your sharp exterior, and you end up in a company where everyone is warm and fuzzy when you'd rather be battling tooth and nail for your commission, neither you nor your employer is going to be happy.

But that doesn't mean you shouldn't be somewhat strategic about your reply. You might say:

I've been told I was too nice for a job before. Because I was trying to impress and was quite bubbly and friendly, they wrongly assumed that I couldn't be assertive. Actually, when it comes to managing a project, I can be quite a strict taskmaster. I think that combination of warmth and high expectations is actually one of my strengths.

Put the interviewer's likely fears to bed by addressing them directly. You could even ask them for their impressions of you, if you feel comfortable doing that, so you can counter any concerns they might have.

47. Can you tell me about a time when you stood up for the right thing to do?

The Real Question: We're not going to end up on the front page of the newspapers for an ethics scandal, are we?

Top-line Tactic: Assure the interviewer that you're honest and trustworthy.

Between the bad behaviour of banks in the run-up to the financial crisis, outrageous executive pay and the high-profile ethics issues of accounting firms in previous years, it's no wonder that surveys consistently show public trust in business declining (though managers take heart – government always fares worse). Companies know that their good name is precious and fragile, and any company worth working for is interested in ensuring that they look after their reputation, along with the good will and trust of their customers.

That means the only right answer to this question is to tell the interviewer about a situation where you proved honest and trustworthy. Never waffle and claim to have avoided ethical quandaries your whole career (recent graduates can draw from their personal and academic experience).

One word of caution, however. As much as companies want you to be ethical, they also need you to be able to work with other people who perhaps have slightly different approaches and boundaries. While you want to come across as upright and dependable, you don't want to seem like an unnecessarily squeaky wheel or someone who can't resolve issues within a team. Make sure, therefore, that your example illustrates how you tried to resolve the dilemma *within your existing team or hierarchy*. Also, what you say should never violate anyone's confidentiality. No one likes a tell-tale unless the violation is truly momentous. Here's one possible example:

When I was a sales manager at Acme I received some new marketing materials for one of our products. They looked great, but when I read through them more closely I could see the marketing department had grossly overstated the capabilities of one of our products. I always like to be honest with my customers, not only because it's the right thing to do, but also because I believe trust is essential for a productive, long-standing relationship. I organized a meeting with marketing and explained that, while the materials were impressive, I felt they were misleading and would create problems for the sales reps down the road. There was a bit of toing and froing, but in the end we ended up with a campaign that worked for everyone.

48. Have you ever stolen a pen from work?

The Real Question: Will you pretend you've never put a foot wrong, or will you do the right thing?

Top-line Tactic: *They're more worried about your integrity than their inventory.*

This a common question – and it's not one you want to be remembered for.

Some people might not regard 'borrowing' a pen as stealing, when strictly speaking it is nothing but stealing, so here the question is being used to obtain insight into your values.

But they're also asking to see if you think the sun shines out of your filing cabinet, because, of course, almost everyone *has* stolen a pen from work. Don't be tempted to fob them off with:

I have once or twice taken a pen from the office in an emergency but I have always returned it the next day or the day after . . .

. . . because the interviewer knows that pen is still on your desk at home, and might challenge you to that effect.

Better to go with something more realistic:

Ha-ha, well, I'd be lying to say I haven't ever absent-mindedly slipped a ballpoint into my jacket pocket, but it usually ends up back on my desk the following day, unless I leave it at home. I haven't got a spare room full of paperclips and staplers, though, if that's what you mean.

It's a question that can draw you into an unnecessary debate on details, so kill the conversation and move on if you can.

49. Did you enjoy school/university?

The Real Question: You have too little experience in the world of work for us to learn about you, so hopefully your academic experience will give us some insight into your character.

Top-line Tactic: *Just as if they were asking about work, be honest but showcase the skills and character traits most relevant to the job.*

If you've been in the workforce for twenty years, this would truly be an odd question to be asked, but recent grads have far fewer professional experiences and accomplishments to discuss. Employers know that, so to get a sense of your character, skills and preferences they'll ask about school or university instead.

The venue of your stories and reflection may be academic rather than professional, but the aim of the interviewer is the same. He or she wants to figure out if your personal style and skills will be a good fit for the role. Therefore the same technique applies to answering this question as to a similarly vague query about previous jobs.

If you're applying for an analyst role that requires you to carefully review data and draw thoughtful conclusions, stress how much you enjoyed the academic side of student life:

What I really loved about being a student was the continuous learning. There were always new challenges to push me to improve and always fresh ideas to get me thinking.

If, on the other hand, you're applying for a PR role that will involve a lot of socializing or, say, a gig as a tour guide, it's a better bet to underline that you were a social butterfly at university (just don't make it sound like you completely ignored the academic side and only went there to have a good time):

I loved university. The courses were interesting, but I particularly enjoyed meeting people from all walks of life, and also all the extracurricular activity on offer. I'm the sort of person who loves to get people together and organize things, so I really enjoyed my work with Habitat for Humanity.

If you're applying for a job as a skilled artisan, there's no need to pretend that you were class boffin if that's neither true nor particularly good preparation for the role under discussion. Just show you were willing to work hard and have mastered the fundamentals:

I'm the sort of person who really enjoys tinkering and making things, so my favourite part of school was my work experience and the practical classes. I made some good friends, and I didn't do too badly in the more academic subjects, but to be honest with you I'm not sorry to be leaving that behind and starting work doing something I really love.

That last part is particularly important. Employers need to hear that you're ready to go to work. Some recent graduates will be secretly considering a career in academia (requiring further study), others will just be horrified at the prospect of starting a full-time job and considering a spot of travel or some other sabbatical. Neither are good long-term bets for an employer, so make sure you tell your interviewer that you've reached the stage in your life when you're ready to put your textbooks and essays aside and get a full-time job. And if you can't say that like you mean it, you're wasting your time and theirs.

50. Do you know anyone at this company?

The Real Question: What will they say about you? Will they try to set me up or give it to me straight?

Top-line Tactic: *If you have connections, be 100 per cent honest about them – but you should also show why you deserve to be hired on merit.*

This question is classified here as a 'character question', for two reasons:

1. If you say you know someone at the company, it's almost certain your interviewer will hunt them down to get a second opinion of, among other things, your character.
2. If you say you don't know anyone at the company *and the interviewer knows that's not true*, your character is again revealed – and your reputation for honesty is sunk.

If you do have inside contacts, the issue of whether to admit it is a vexed one. On one hand, you don't want to appear as though you've been overly coached by an insider, since the interviewer might feel that they're being gamed, or at least not interviewing the real you. There is also the risk that your acquaintance is not well respected in the organization.

On the other hand, it's never good to pretend you're a total outsider when you're not. Quite apart from being morally wrong, there is every chance that your contact will have mentioned you to the interviewer at some point in the past – many industries are small enough for that to be a realistic prospect.

And even if you and your ally can keep your prior relationship under wraps, you'll have to keep up that pretence for as long as all three of you work there.

Far better, then, to come clean about whom you know, but to play down their importance:

I know a couple of your staff, actually, and we've spoken in general terms about my coming here, but that wouldn't affect how I'd approach the job – I've got my own ideas about that.

51. How do you maintain a good work/life balance?

The Real Question: If we hire you, will you be here when we need you? Or are you rapidly going to become a stressed-out, burnt-out mess?

Top-line Tactic: *They really don't care about how you keep work apart from your home life; they want to know how you keep your home life and stress away from your work.*

The most common advice you're likely to hear about work/life balance and interviews is *don't discuss it*.

Expert after expert will warn candidates about bringing up work/life balance during an interview, as hiring managers generally read such queries as evidence of laziness and a desire to clock out as soon as the second hand hits five o'clock. But what if it's the interviewer who is bringing up work/life balance?

Don't be fooled. Chances are good that you haven't simply stumbled on the nicest company in the world, who will be genuinely concerned you don't ever miss your kid's football game or your long-standing Thursday-evening happy hour. Employers aren't evil, but they are self-interested. If they are asking about work/life balance, chances are they want to be reassured that you can juggle all the stresses and responsibilities in your life without deterioration in your on-the-job performance or rapid burnout.

To this end, reassure the interviewer that you have systems in place to deal with stress and scheduling conflicts, and that the pressures of home will not at all impinge on your ability to do the job.

For me, weekends are really important. I think it's essential to find some time to completely switch off and recuperate, so that on Monday morning you're refreshed and ready to go. That often means a long hike or getting out of doors somehow, which I find is a great stress reliever – I even get some of my best ideas on long rambles. I also try to take a quick walk in the park at lunch if I can because I find it clears my mind and helps me perform at my best in the afternoon. Small things like that have really helped me keep burnout at bay over my ten-year career. Plus, a shared calendar with my partner and a really helpful mother-in-law nearby certainly don't hurt either.

52. Are your grades a good indicator of success in this business?

The Real Question: Did you make the correct academic choices? Were your results good enough and do you take responsibility for them?

Top-line Tactic: *If you don't have excellent results to brag about, explain your academic performance without blaming others or sounding defensive.*

This might not sound like the nicest question you could be asked, but it's actually a less aggressive version of other questions about academic performance. The interviewer could be asking you 'Why are your grades so low?' or 'Are you over-qualified' or 'Do you really think your philosophy degree is good preparation for the world of work?' etc. So take a moment to appreciate that this is the grades question you happened to get.

If the interviewer goes with this more neutral formulation of the grades question, they're probably trying to learn how you felt about academia and how you approached your time in education, as well gauging your ability to talk sensibly about shortcomings and trade-offs, and less about how you performed at school (which is probably on your CV anyway).

Answering is easy enough if you have excellent grades to boast of. Just highlight your most relevant accomplishments – without bragging unattractively. Perhaps that could sound like this:

I do feel it was good preparation. My maths degree will obviously help me out as I start my career as a financial analyst, but it's actually the study skills and the ability to keep at it even if a problem is really tough that I think will serve me best.

If, on the other hand, you don't have the sort of results that will wow the interviewer, you need to tread carefully. You don't want to come across as defensive about your less-than-stellar performance lest the interviewer suspect you lack confidence. Nor do you want to blame circumstance or cast yourself as the victim – every employer is looking for team members who will be accountable for their performance.

A better approach is to highlight the trade-offs you made and the aspects of your time at school or university that show you in the best light. You may have barely passed chemistry, but maybe you were a club leader, completed several impressive internships, or spent a good deal of time gaining actual work experience while at university.

I didn't get the excellent results I wanted in all my subjects, but I don't think that's going to affect how well I do here. Also, I learned other skills at university during my stint as the president of the Entrepreneur Society and working at the university radio station, which was a lot of fun and really taught me to think on my feet and connect with a wide variety of people. Course results are important, but they're not the only thing you can gain from further education.

53. Would you rather be liked or feared?

The Real Question: What's your leadership style? Also, do you have the poise to wriggle out of a trick question?

Top-line Tactic: *Opt for the unsaid option – 'respected'.*

This question is definitely one of those moral dilemmas I mentioned in the introduction to this chapter. In these circumstances, it's OK to dodge the options given and choose another adjective, so long as you've first made a stab at answering the question one way or the other. In this case, your best bet is to opt for the unstated possibility of 'respected'. Just make sure you start out by acknowledging the original framing of the question before avoiding the given options. That might sound something like this:

*Hmmm, well I certainly wouldn't want to be feared. I think fear is a ter-
rible motivator: people are often feared because they're irrational and
acting for personal and unpredictable reasons. I definitely don't operate
that way and I wouldn't like anyone to think I did.*

*Everyone wants to be liked, but I don't think being liked per se is
enough. You can like someone and still think they're no good at their job.
Also, sometimes you need to do unpopular things to get the job done. I'd
sooner aim to be respected. That's a good mix of personal connection –
being liked; the ability to get done what's necessary – being feared; and
making my co-workers understand that I do whatever's best for the
team as a whole.*

54. What are your thoughts on the interview process so far?

The Real Question: How are your diplomacy skills?

Top-line Tactic: *Walk the line between flattery and criticism.*

At first glance this is a truly weird question. The interviewer
couldn't possibly be trying to work on their interview skills
by soliciting a little feedback during the interview, and your
answer couldn't be in any way relevant to the job at hand,
could it? But maybe in a sort of sneaky way, it could.

While your ability to critique your interviewer is highly
unlikely to be an essential skill should you get the job, the
ability to offer constructive feedback while maintaining pleasant relations with colleagues almost certainly will come in
handy. In all likelihood that's the essential political skill your
interviewer is trying to test here.

A more straightforward way to ask this question might be:
Critique this process [and/or me] *in a way that shows you can be*

diplomatic. A good answer will balance the need to be truthful and constructive (i.e. avoid pointless and obvious flattery) with the need to show respect and ensure the interviewer continues to like you. It's OK to express a little surprise – this is an unusual question, after all – but then proceed by keeping calm, maintaining your poise and channelling your inner diplomat to come up with an accurate but pleasant assessment of the ongoing process. Note the answer below finishes with a question. Not many interviewers will mark you down for asking them a question, especially not if you've answered their original question. Asking them a question will allow you to bail out of this difficult conversation long before it hits the ground and bursts into flames.

Well, I enjoyed the fact that we started off with a little tour of the facility on the way to the conference room and I definitely think you've done a great job of examining my job-specific skills. I really had to dig deep and think carefully when you quizzed me on how I'd handle the quality control issues you've been facing, which pushed me to get into the nitty-gritty of how I work and also gave me a better idea of the challenges I'd be facing should I be offered the job. I don't think we've discussed my work style and the culture of the team I'd be joining as much, however. I'd love to get into how the team interacts and how I'd fit in. Is that something we'll be talking about later in the interview process?

55. Why should I choose you over other candidates?

The Real Question: You probably have the skills to do this job, but what sort of person are you? What intangibles will you bring to the company?

Top-line Tactic: *Skip the competencies here and instead focus on what sets you apart as a person.*

This question gets candidates rattled. When you don't even know the other candidates, how on earth are you supposed to compare yourself to them? The trick to keeping your cool here is to forget the comparison framing, and simply take the question as an opportunity to expand on your finest personal characteristics.

Obviously, interviewers ask this question because they want to see what sets you apart from everyone else, but chances are their main concern isn't your competencies. You've already been selected for interview. No hiring manager gives up their time for a candidate they don't believe can do the job based on their CV. So what they want to hear when they ask this is what you can bring aside from your skills. What are the most interesting facets of you as a person that aren't captured in the work experience section of your CV?

This is a chance to highlight the intangibles you haven't been able to work into the conversation up to this point. Essentially, you've just been given the go-ahead to brag a little about yourself. Take the opportunity – just don't go wildly overboard with the self-praise. Consider something along these lines:

I'm a person who likes learning and continually improving. I have a natural curiosity. I like getting out of my comfort zone and try to do whatever I'm doing as well as I can. I'm self-motivated and flexible – in a working environment there's a need to adapt and if it means having to run a training course then I'll do it; if it means covering the floor I'll do it; if it means motivating the team, I'll do it. I also look at my other colleagues because they may have skills that I don't and I'm not afraid to ask for help. I'm extremely dedicated to my work and I think that's something that's part of my personality. Also I'm very honest and if you ask me something I will give you my sincere opinion, whether I think it's what you want to hear or not. I feel like honesty is something you've got – it's like a lapel badge. I like people to come to me because they know I'm going to give them a straight answer.

This is also a good opportunity to stress skills you have that are unusual for a candidate applying for this sort of position, or special abilities that have not yet been discussed in depth in the interview. The idea is to sell yourself as offering a unique package of abilities to the employer. Perhaps something like:

I'm sure I'm not the only one who understands this software, but I believe I'm also great at putting complex, technical concepts into everyday language, and I think that's pretty rare among technical people.

Or:

All the candidates you're interviewing no doubt have the requisite child-care experience, but as I studied in Paris for a year, I also speak fluent French, which I used to create fun and educational language lessons at my current job. Both the kids and the parents loved it.

If you hear this question, you can definitely see it as a positive sign about how the interview is progressing. If they bother to ask you something along these lines, they probably think you can do the job and simply want to determine if they'll like doing it with you. Lots of people can perform the job, but what is it about you that will make the interviewer want to hire you?

56. Is it OK to spend time at work on non-work stuff, like Facebook or YouTube?

The Real Question: Are you coming here to work or play?

Top-line Tactic: *Their house, their rules. If you don't like it, don't take their money.*

Nothing gets older employers foaming at the mouth quite like the topic of workplace distraction, also known as a morbid and sometimes irrational fear of millennials looking at YouTube all day, on the employer's time.

In truth, it's not just millennials who are bunking off in the office. Pretty much everyone is, although the issue is best illustrated by the gulf between boomers and digital natives, not least because the baby-boomer demographic holds most of the money and power in the developed world. Consequently their views on this are best not ignored, even if they're not universally accepted.

As the employer sees it, you are not paid to look at YouTube videos of cats falling into custard. But go into any office and it'll often seem that some people do little else.

Certainly, there is a great deal of research to back up the fear that workplaces have become giant hubs of bunking off, with everything from Facebook to porn being fair use of bandwidth to some. And the data for this research usually comes straight from the pipes and, as such, can't be challenged: there really *is* a lot of bunking off going on. One study into browsing habits, from ContentWatch, quoted by *Forbes* magazine, put it like this:

- Baby Boomers: born between 1946 and 1964 – waste 41 minutes a day at work.
- Gen X'ers: born between 1965 and 1981 – waste 1.6 hours a day at work.
- Millennials: born between 1982 and 2004 – waste 2 hours a day at work.

For their part, nothing makes young people fume more than the thought of being forcibly separated from their social browsing during the working day. As a millennial sees it, they've managed to get *this* far in life by seamlessly combining their browsing habits with their external obligations, so there is no harm in them multitasking their way through the rest of their career either.

So how much browsing is too much? Well . . . *you can forget trying to come up with a number*. Here, the number is not the important thing.

Instead, you ought to be seen to accept that the issue is hugely important to employers, and that any time you spend doing something other than what you're being paid to do is likely to be viewed as misconduct, regardless of whether you think that's reasonable or not. In short, you need to abide by whatever workplace policies are in effect.

Your employer doesn't want to be reminded that everyone bunks off now and again. They already know – it's why they're bringing it up with you in the first place – so you've nothing to gain from being seen to consider both sides of the issue.

You're being offered money in exchange for a certain set of specified behaviours; if you take the money but don't deliver on the behaviours, you're being dishonourable. In most workplaces, social browsing is explicitly banned or severely restricted. If you think that's an unreasonable demand for an employer to make, don't take their money.

57. What are three positive things your boss/ colleagues would say about you?

The Real Question: What's your track record, really? Are you self-aware? Are you going to sound like all the rest?

Top-line Tactic: *Show, don't tell.*

For this question more than most, it's important to deliver your answer in a natural and relaxed tone. That's because a good interviewer will be on guard against those candidates who are better at getting jobs than doing them. These candidates (feel free to award them your own nickname) are rare but can be highly destructive to an organization. They're tough to spot, too. Peer feedback is one way to root them out, so when the subject of peer feedback comes up, you'd better be ready to say something that feels true and accurate to you – that way your tone of voice will act as a guarantor to your words.

It's said the ability to take a compliment is a sign that you've reached a certain level of maturity, and sure enough not many people can do it. And the ability to *pay yourself* a compliment, without sounding boastful or fraudulent, is a sign of still greater maturity, so it follows that hardly anyone can do that either. Most of us must practise it. A very modest candidate might not want to praise themselves for too long without eventually pulling the pin on some self-criticism, but the question isn't asking you for self-criticism: just the good stuff.

The best way to talk about yourself is to say what you've *done*, rather than who you are. Your personal qualities will be inferred from your achievements. If your boss might truthfully say that you were the highest-performing sales rep last year, it's easier to cite that fact with conviction than to say 'I'm great at sales', and it's much more useful to the interviewer too. Quantifiable achievement will always beat self-serving rhetoric.

If the interviewer presses you to talk about your personal qualities and not your professional achievements, it's essential that you avoid obvious terms like 'hard-working' or 'conscientious' or 'entrepreneurial'. Recruitment consultants all attest that simply *everyone* uses the same few words when asked to describe themselves in a job interview. In fact, overused interview words are the subject of many an annual survey. Here are ten overused words from LinkedIn's annual survey in 2013:

responsible
strategic
creative
effective
patient
expert
organizational
driven
innovative
analytical

If you use these words during an interview you're simply putting yourself back in the crowd.

Technology means we all have a thesaurus in our pocket these days, so you've no excuse not to dig out some lesser-known words. It would be pretentious if you spoke using only rare words but, if the interviewer is asking you to name personal qualities, your priority is to separate yourself from

everyone else. (You can be confident that the other candidates won't be trying hard in this respect: ask any glazed-over
recruiter.)

It's not hard to do:

- You're determined? Nope – you're *stoical* (you endure
  pain and hardship without showing your feelings or
  complaining).
- You're entrepreneurial? Nope – you're *comfortable with risk
  and uncertainty*.
- You're conscientious? Nope – you're *meticulous*.

Obviously you can't answer this question unless you've
made an honest inventory of your personal and professional
achievements. If taking stock proves difficult – or, more
likely, if you're too modest in your stocktake – *ask* someone
what they would say about you. That exercise can throw up
funny responses from well-meaning friends, which might
lighten the proceedings.

58. What has been the biggest setback in your career?

The Real Question: Are you resilient? Are you honest?

Top-line Tactic: Be frank about your failure but positive about
what you learned.

Your first reaction to this question is probably an inward
groan. Of course no one likes to dwell on his or her failures,
but try not to be too down on questions like this. It's best to
view the interviewer's attempts to probe your setbacks not as

sadism or an attempt to trip you up, but rather as a chance to demonstrate two extremely valuable characteristics – frankness and resilience.

The secret to acing this sort of tricky question is to strike a balance between light and dark. Don't say you've never had one. Instead, speak honestly about a real setback, but also accentuate the positive aspects of the experience – how resilient you were in the face of failure and what you learned from the experience, even if it's simply that you won't be making the same mistake again.

The interviewer cares far more about how you responded to adversity than the particular circumstance you faced. Ultimately, you want to present the setback as evidence of both your humility and a lesson learned on someone else's watch that has made you stronger. For this reason, it's not necessary to bore your questioner with the particulars of your failure. Just give an overview, such as:

At my last job, I was asked to manage a large project. We worked with consultants to create a project plan and estimate costs, but when we presented our plan to the CEO, he wanted a major change. I could see what he wanted would never work, but I was too scared to speak up in that meeting and say so.

So we tried to accommodate the CEO's request and it was a disaster. However, being on that project taught me two valuable lessons: first, speak up when you think something is wrong – at least it shows you're paying attention and it could avoid a potentially serious problem. Second, I now know how to avoid the sunk-cost fallacy, where good money is thrown at a problem in the false hope that it will somehow rectify an inherent flaw.

Younger job seekers or recent graduates may not yet have experienced a significant career setback. Be honest about this with your interviewer but try to offer an example from your education or work experience that conveys the same message of perseverance and your ability to snatch something positive from a negative situation.

59. Your boss overslept and is now late for a client meeting. He calls and asks you to tell the client that he is stuck in traffic – in other words to lie for him. What do you do?

The Real Question: How do you make difficult decisions? Who's more important – a client or a boss? Do you value the team or the rules? What are your standards?

Top-line Tactic: *Very gently undermine the question. Say that you've been presented with an impossible situation and so no one should expect a perfect answer.*

So, your interviewer has posed a hypothetical dilemma – unlucky you! You can't win. On one hand, everyone knows that you ought to keep your boss happy. Equally, everyone knows you shouldn't lie to anyone, let alone a client. So, will you snitch on your boss, on whom your career depends in part, or will you lie to the client, the person who justifies your commercial existence?

This rather loaded language ought to reveal that dilemma questions can sometimes be rather artificial, to the point of silliness. Sadly, you've got to say *something*.

So how do you answer? Before you begin, consider that dilemmas are designed to be 100 per cent impossible to answer without you appearing morally dubious in some way.

To know that is to know your answer. Take the sting out of the question by highlighting its impossible nature.

You might suggest that your answer will inevitably be slightly unsatisfactory, and that real life usually offers more wiggle room.

First of all, if the situation really is exactly as you describe then I'm in trouble either way, because it's wrong to lie and it's wrong to disobey your boss. So, the best I'd be able to do is ring the client, apologize profusely and explain that my boss had been delayed, without saying by what. I'd probably ask if the client would prefer to rearrange the meeting, which might in any case be the best outcome for my boss. Certainly, if we're running late then we owe the client his time back, and its important the client hears us admit it. Beyond that, I'm really not sure. I've never been in that situation.

Bottom line: treat people as you want to be treated. No one wants to be lied to. That's the best answer I can give here.

FIVE

COMPETENCY QUESTIONS

Competency questions, such as *Tell me about a time you've worked to a deadline*, are very popular among certain types of interviewer, notably professionalized interviewers (e.g. recruitment consultants and HR people) and among public sector organizations, which are often obliged to recruit in a more prescribed and box-ticking fashion than their private sector counterparts.

Competency questions are so popular that there is no hiding from them. Instead of being asked to speculate on what they would do in a given situation, the candidate is asked to give specific examples of situations that have already occurred. That makes a world of difference. Competency questions are usually catnip to people who can do the job and kryptonite to those who just talk a good game – more or less the opposite of open-ended questions. An experienced interviewer will know this and balance out the interview with both open-ended and competency questions.

Assuming you actually have the required competencies, competency-based questions are very straightforward to answer. There are a number of acronyms for remembering how, but by far the most common is the STAR technique, where you give context to the Situation, the Task, your Actions and the Result.

In our section on competency questions, not everything you read might fit everyone's definition of what a competency question is, but I've grouped these questions together because at heart they all deal with the same issue, namely: *How well will you do the job in hand?*

Often contrary to appearances, at the heart of what interviewers are trying to find out is *whether you will be able to do the job you're applying for*. For each job there are a list of qualities that are prerequisites to do just that. These questions are used to find out if you possess these qualities.

60. What was the last big decision you had to make?

The Real Question: How do you think through problems? Is your approach appropriate for this role?

Top-line Tactic: *Give the interviewer a window into your decision-making process, stressing the particular type of reasoning that is most important for the job at hand.*

Everyone makes tough decisions at work, but not everyone makes them the same way. This question is designed to get inside your head and figure out *how* you reason and weigh alternatives.

Answering should be fairly straightforward: be honest, pick a recent choice you made and talk the interviewer through the decision and your thought process in a clear, succinct manner.

Much depends on the sort of role you're applying for. Is

this a management position that requires an iron nerve to balance business objectives and human concerns? Choose an example of a time you had to weigh those trade-offs.

I had to decide whether to end a relationship with one of our suppliers. We'd worked together for years but the quality of the components they supplied had been declining for quite a while. We'd warned them several times, but there had been no improvement. I had a good working relationship with my contact and I knew that terminating the contract would be a blow to the firm, but my first priority had to be our customers, so after researching the alternatives I changed suppliers. It was a hard decision to make because I knew I was affecting other people's livelihoods, but I still think it was the right way to go.

Are they looking for a maths whiz to crunch numbers? In that case your best bet is to choose a situation where you made a data-driven decision. Pick a decision that allows you to highlight your quantitative skills as well as your ability to apply them in a complex human context.

The idea here is to select a decision you made in a domain that emphasizes the key type of decision making for the role you're applying for. That may entail stressing your empathy and strong sense of people's quirks, your analytical chops, your stomach for tough calls, your ability to think about the bigger picture, your coolness under time pressure, or your intuitive grasp of questions of design, branding or aesthetics. As always, if you find yourself struggling to fill out a hypothetical answer, the job spec will show you the way forward.

61. Tell me about a time you've worked to/ missed a deadline

The Real Question: How do you prioritize tasks, organize your work and handle time pressure?

Top-line Tactic: *Apply the STAR technique, but be human.*

In this section of the book, you'll probably very quickly notice a pattern: lots of these questions start with *Tell me about a time you . . .* If you find your interviewer is using lots of this type of question, it's a clear sign that you're dealing with what's known as a competency-based interview.

The idea animating this technique is that specific past examples are a better gauge of a candidate's likely future performance than general assertions about skills. So if you want to know if someone handles time pressure well, it's better to elicit a story about a time they worked under a tight deadline than it is to ask point blank, *How do you cope under pressure?*

The theory is simple, but if you're expecting a more traditional interview style, a competency-based approach can throw you. Don't let the apparently open-ended nature of these questions rattle you. There is a simple, structured technique to help you organize your response.

In the introduction to this chapter I mentioned the STAR acronym: Situation, Task, Action, Results. (Alternatively, some experts use CAR, swapping 'Context' for 'Situation/Task'. They pretty much amount to the same thing.) Here's how to use the technique to shape your answers:

- **Situation/Task (or Context):** Explain whatever background the interviewer needs to understand the story you're about to tell. What's the situation you were facing? What tasks did you need to undertake to resolve it? Include how important or difficult the situation was as well as any constraints on your actions. Make sure you're crystal clear about your goal. Think of this as 'setting the scene'.

Example: At Acme Ltd, I was responsible for representing the firm at trade shows. My second year there, it happened that three events we usually attended were scheduled within a month of each other – generally they were spread out over a much longer period. It meant a tremendous amount of work was compressed into a really tight window. These shows were a huge source of lead generation for the company, so it was essential we attended and presented our products in the best light.

- **Actions:** What concrete actions did you take to resolve the situation? You always want to present yourself as the driver of the successful outcome. Don't hog credit, but never cast yourself as in need of rescue or the victim of circumstance. Always consider what skills the interviewer is probably looking for and try to illustrate those.

Example: I enjoy a challenge, but I took a long, hard look at the situation and realized preparing all three up to the standards I'd want was going be impossible, so I had to prioritize. One was much less relevant to us than the other two, so I agreed with my manager that we'd focus on only those two. Once that was settled, I could draw up a detailed to-do list with interim deadlines for each item so that I'd have all the materials I needed to really represent the company well.

- **Results:** What was the outcome of the event? Remember, everyone likes a happy ending, and in business they like a quantifiable happy ending even better.

Example: The two events went off without a hitch and I was able to bring several really solid leads back to our sales department. One of them actually resulted in a £100,000 contract, so in the end I was pleased I'd decided to drop the third one.

As you can see, impressing at a competency-based interview is all about the story you pick and your ability to furnish convincing, concrete details, so it is particularly important to prepare for this sort of interview. The above example is a winner as it showcases the underlying abilities the interviewer is likely to be interested in when asking the question: organizational ability, skill at prioritizing and coolness under pressure.

Don't shy away from including a bit of adversity or failure. It humanizes you and helps convince the listener of your sincerity. All jobs involve difficulties. The interviewer is trying to figure out how you'll handle them.

A final word of wisdom about STAR: as a structured system, it can help guide your answers and calm your nerves, but follow it robotically and you will risk appearing canned or stiff. Make sure that while you're hitting each key section, you're doing so in a natural, conversational way. Again, practice can help.

62. Tell me about a big change you've had to deal with

The Real Question: When the change happened, did you shrink from it or did you lean into it? Do you still have the energy for change? What mark would you give your adaptability, out of ten?

Top-line Tactic: Show that you think of change as a permanent and necessary fixture, not as an occasional obstacle.

Sadly, you can no longer get brownie points for observing that the world changes very quickly these days. Everybody knows about rapid change: they see it everywhere. Besides, this particular question is a competency question. That means the interviewer wants to hear times, places, names and outcomes, not a big-picture sermon about this funny old world we live in.

Fortunately, nobody's career is without change. You'll easily be able to go in with several examples, not just one. Your top line in any of these examples is to show that you *think of change as an opportunity to grow, not an ordeal to endure*.

A good answer begins by acknowledging the specific, positive results of the change and then working backwards in time to the bad old days.

When the government introduced health-and-safety exams for construction workers, it was always clear we'd end up with fewer accidents on site, and better workers too. But as the site foreman, I had to tell skilled workers I'd known for twenty years that it was time for them to go back to school, else they'd be off the job. Some of them didn't like that, and I can understand why. The guy who protested the most turned out to be a technophobe. He'd heard the exam was computer-based, so I showed him that the exam wasn't really about computers, just a bit of point-and-click software, easy to use. He passed. And nobody on my site left because of the exams, though lots elsewhere did.

You have to work out why people oppose change, and sometimes it's not the reason they give you. If there were no changes in my job, I'd do something else. And I visit fewer colleagues in hospital these days.

This answer shows you:

- being open to new experiences;
- soldiering on through the bad atmosphere change often creates;
- getting into the minds of those who oppose change, many of whom are often just scared, not lazy or boring.

It helps if you can cite an example of change at the hiring firm, and relate your answer to that. Look in the press release and news section of the firm's website: there you'll find examples of change that the firm is probably pleased to talk about.

It also helps to show that change never stopped you from focusing on the ultimate purpose of your job, that the little things don't matter to you. For example, airline cabin crew used to be a glamorous vocation. It isn't glamorous any more, but that's got nothing to do with getting people off a plane in an emergency, which, despite appearances, has always principally been what cabin crew are paid to do.

For maximum impact, give an example of when you've *volunteered* for change, such as taking a discretionary professional development course.

63. Tell me about a time you've had to persuade someone to do something

The Real Question: People are tricky creatures. Do you know how to handle them?

Top-line Tactic: *Focus on how you persuaded people, not just that you managed to convince them.*

We've been through several of these competency-based *Tell me about a time you . . .* type questions already, so you might ask what's different about this one? It's a good point – the basic mechanics of the STAR method remain the same for all of these, so what's left to consider after you have that mastered?

The next level of analysis is simply to consider the competencies behind the question. What quality or skills is the interviewer hoping to see you demonstrate in your answer? Here, for instance, this question about persuasion is a classic attempt to gauge people skills. The interviewer is probably looking for competencies like:

- empathy
- charm or rapport building
- confidence and possibly assertiveness
- flexibility
- ability to handle conflict/difficult conversations
- ability to put your ego aside, humility
- ability to understand and motivate others

Of course, the exact skills required vary depending on the role and company culture, so take a moment before answering to think about what abilities the interviewer wants to see. Then use STAR to weave an answer that demonstrates them, for example:

When I was at ABC I was managing a group of six designers. Several of them came to me asking for more flexibility in their schedule and whether they could work from home occasionally. I'd done some research into productivity and I knew that creative people often benefit from this sort of freedom, but that management is often reluctant to give it them. In order to persuade my director, I put together a small presentation from the management literature that included several studies on the effectiveness of flexible work programmes, their positive impact on hiring and retention, and best practices for running them.

I knew my boss would be worrying about productivity, so I came up with some key indicators we could track to hopefully counter that concern. I arranged a meeting with the director and also roped in HR, because they would need to approve the policy change. My boss wasn't wild about the plan, but I stuck to my guns and ran through all the facts, countering each of his objections. He said he was impressed with my preparation and would think about it. After a week, I got the go-ahead to implement the change. My team was over the moon, and not only did productivity rise 20 per cent, but soon after that I was able to hire a truly stellar designer, who said one of the main draws of the job was the flexible schedule.

Notice that this answer doesn't simply tick the 'ability to persuade' box but delves deeper into *how* the candidate went about persuading others, highlighting key constituent skills like empathy (foreseeing the director's objections), consultation (roping in HR and listening to the designers) and tenacity (sticking with the debate despite objections).

64. Give me an example of something you've tried in your job that hasn't worked. How did you learn from it?

The Real Question: Are you too afraid of failure to be innovative?

Top-line Tactic: *Don't mistake this question for one about setbacks or failure. It's about your willingness to experiment.*

Ostensibly, this question looks similar to other questions that ask candidates to own up to a failure, but if you think the interviewer is primarily interested in getting at your weaknesses here, you've most likely misunderstood his or her intent.

There is a distinction between drawn-out failure and fast, productive experimentation (which, by its nature, will often result in failure). Companies definitely don't like it when projects to which they've devoted huge quantities of resources end up not paying off, but many do want you to try new things, even if that means those ideas sometimes fall flat. Grey New York, a unit of leading advertising agency WPP, even offers a 'Heroic Failure' award to encourage risk-taking and innovation.

Tor Myhren, the Worldwide Chief Creative Officer of the unit, explained to the *Wall Street Journal* that the unconventional award was a response to his sense that his people were growing more conservative. 'I thought rewarding a little risk-taking was potentially an answer,' he told the paper. Myhren isn't the only one trying this approach. SurePayroll offers a 'Best New Mistake' award while gaming company Supercell celebrates each failure with champagne.

What's the point of these examples? If your interviewer asks about things you 'tried that didn't work', they're probably probing to see if you understand that taking risks and occasionally failing are part of creativity – and whether you're too much of a perfectionist to allow yourself to be innovative. The right answer, then, isn't to play down your missteps, but to play up the fact that you try new things, rapidly assess if they're working and move on if they aren't. Show you're willing to take risks and experiment to improve your work.

I think it's really important to experiment and try new things at work. Of course they don't always work out, but you can usually learn something valuable in the process. It's just important to pilot new initiatives to limit the costs.

When I was running the customer service department at XYZ, for example, I spoke to several potential clients who said they were considering signing up for our services but were put off by the fact they had to commit to a year-long contract. I spoke to the team about it and we decided to offer a month-by-month payment plan. We also discussed how we would measure success and I kept careful track of the costs and revenue from the new option. We soon found out that customers who weren't committed enough for an annual contract often only stuck around for a few months and the additional administrative costs of managing these short-term accounts were higher than the returns of the additional business. We ended the experiment after about six months, but the experience taught us to stick firmly to longer-term contracts, and that quality was better than quantity when it came to our customers.

65. Tell me about a time you've disagreed with a senior member of staff

The Real Question: When it comes to office politics are you going to be a pot stirrer or can you work through disagreements in a mature, productive way? We don't want playground drama around here.

Top-line Tactic: *Show you can debate like an adult for the betterment of the business, by responding openly and honestly.*

No one ever says in an interview: 'I'm a handful! If there's an office feud, juicy piece of gossip or long-held grudge going on, I'm probably a part of it.'

Interviewers know that and so have found subtler ways than direct questions to figure out how you handle conflict and whether you can maintain a healthy separation between the personal and the professional. This question is one of those ways.

The success of your answer depends as much on tone as content. You're looking to convey the warmth, understanding, rationality and professionalism with which you deal with your disagreements in the way you answer the question. Stay well away from political struggles, hurt feelings or battles over territory or influence. Instead, offer an example of professional people sitting down together to arrive at an answer to a contentious business question. Stress your ability to fight your corner in a constructive way that utilizes evidence and emotional intelligence.

I had a disagreement over sales strategy in my last job. I used to generate leads on the phone, but management wanted us to change tactics and go out to sell on foot. For me that wasn't the best use of my time. I thought we should establish a connection first through phone calls, then develop a tailored marketing solution for our best prospects. Also, it was quite a big firm, and I thought going door to door wouldn't present the right image.

I said I thought there was a better way of doing things and asked whether they really wanted us to be seen as a door-to-door sales company as opposed to a professional outfit that would quantify an opportunity before going out to act on it. Management let me trial my approach and it worked, so they implemented it across the regional sales force. I'd only been there for two and a half months at the time, so I thought twice before saying anything, but I was sure that applying a methodical structure to the problem would increase productivity and in the end I was proved right.

66. If offered the job, what would be your first priority or thing you would change?

The Real Question: Can you strike a good balance between consultation and initiative? Are you going to charge in and step on toes?

Top-line Tactic: *Decide how much initiative/change the company is looking for and pitch your answer accordingly.*

The most important word in this question is 'or'. Talking about priorities or changes you would make are two very different things. The former can be applied to any position and is more about how you'll approach getting acclimatized. The latter focuses on shaking up the status quo and is often most appropriate for management-level positions or situations where the organization is actively looking for change. Your first task here is to figure out which side of the 'or' is more appropriate for this particular position.

Priorities

For roles that are less about leading change and more about individual performance, your answer should emphasize how you plan to get yourself up to speed in your new job. No matter how much you probe, you'll never know exactly what you're walking into, so answers that focus on acclimatization are a safe bet. You could include:

175

- Getting to know your co-workers.
- Learning about the customers.
- Investigating the company's products or services.

If you're quite familiar with the role, as well as the company and its products, there are several general priorities you can cite. As always, it's best to back up your ability to tackle these challenges with evidence from your past experience. This might sound something like:

- **Add value:** *In my first month, I'd love to focus on kick-starting that key project we discussed earlier. In my last job I tackled something similar, so I think I could really add value immediately by taking the following steps . . .*
- **Make a colleague's job easier:** *In my last job I was able to really improve candidate tracking for the HR executives I was supporting by implementing a new workflow. I'm hoping to be able to put that experience to use here straight away to save my new colleagues a lot of worry and time wasted on administrative work.*
- **Make more money:** *In my last job I was able to save our department 15 per cent annually on contractor costs by reviewing our existing contracts and streamlining things so we were dealing with only four contractors rather than seven. So one of my first priorities would be to take a look at the contractors your company is using to see if I could make similar savings.*

Changes

If you're specifically asked to do a turnaround job, are being brought in to innovate, or otherwise get the sense that the role is about making changes, go ahead and highlight some areas that strike you as in need of work, but be cautious, this is a loaded question.

No one likes a know-it-all who barges in and disregards the experience and opinions of their new co-workers, so make sure that when you suggest areas for improvement, you don't come across as high-handed. Stress consultation and the need for information gathering. Words like *evolve*, *examine*, *contribute* and *develop* can be more effective than *change*, *overhaul*, *transform* or *fix*. You're trying to get across that you'll bring ideas to the table, not that you're a bully.

On the other hand, initiative is a key skill for managers, so don't completely dodge the question – your answer should contain a few substantive issues you're keen to dig into straight away.

67. Why are you a good fit for the company?

The Real Question: Do you just want a job, any job, or are you specifically interested in us?

Top-line Tactic: *Arm yourself with knowledge about the company, so you can offer evidence to prove you'll fit right in.*

(A brief note: The emphasis here could be on *you* or *the company*, meaning the main thrust of the question could be either selling yourself or explaining your motivation to join this firm in particular. There's some overlap, of course, but you'll have to play it by ear. If you think the question is mostly about your unique selling points see *Why should I choose you over other candidates?* (p. 151). For what to say when the focus is on your motivation to join this specific organization, read on below.)

Everyone wants to be wanted. What goes for your next date for a Friday night goes for the company that you're interviewing with as well. If you picked someone for a night of potential romance, only to tell the person you randomly selected him or her because you thought they might answer your email, he or she is not going to be very impressed. Neither will the interviewer if you can't provide a seductive answer to this question. The best answers offer a solid motivation for your interest in this specific job.

Being a long-time fan of the company and/or its product or having a long-standing passion for the sector is obviously an ideal foundation. It gets a little harder if you're changing career trajectory, unfamiliar with the firm or new to the job market, but fear not: you can hack your way to a plausible answer to this question with a little preparation.

Take some time before the interview to look at the company's social media presence, for example. This should give you insight into the organization's personality, as can poking around their website. Pay particular attention to their mission statement or values. Try to get a sense of their culture and what this company believes makes them stand out.

Once you have all this information, you have a blueprint. You can look at your own skills, accomplishments and personality and tie them in with what the organization is known for. This shows you've done your homework and offers another opportunity to highlight why you're the right person to solve the interviewer's problems:

My background is in a similar field, as you can see from my CV, and I've been keeping my skills sharp and learning about the latest technology. I've always taken all the professional development opportunities I've been offered, and I'm happy to learn more. I know you're an organization that really values staying on the cutting edge of technology. I was really impressed with some of the technical details I read about the XYZ project, for instance. There's a good fit between my interest in evolving my skills and the fact that your firm is known for continual technical improvements.

Be warned, it is easy to give an answer that sounds canned. Truly over-the-top enthusiasm is likely to be viewed with a degree of suspicion (especially if it's not backed up with evidence on your CV), as is a too-perfect alignment between their website copy and your professed passions. This is one answer you don't want to oversell.

68. What was the last thing you taught?

The Real Question: Will you be a good coach to your direct reports and teammates?

Top-line Tactic: *Show the interviewer that hiring you means getting not only your skills, but enhanced performance out of your colleagues as well.*

Everyone likes a two-for-one sale, and that goes for companies too. It's great to convince your interviewer that, should you be hired, you'll bring important skills to the organization, but it's even better if you can put across that you will upgrade your colleagues' skills as well.

This question is most likely to be asked of candidates for managerial positions, but the ability to teach laterally as well as down is highly valued as well, so you could face this question no matter what role you are applying for. As with all competency questions, good answers are truthful, detailed when it comes to your actions, and focused on positive outcomes. Here's one example:

My job title is customer service representative, but it's really half handling customer requests over the phone and half admin work, processing and tracking orders. The company recently hired someone with a strong

*administrative background, but less experience interacting with custom-
ers. She mastered the admin in no time, but I noticed that she was
often struggling to handle customers, especially when they were
unhappy or agitated. She sometimes got quite upset, which wasn't helping anyone.*

*I could sympathize, because it took me a while to learn the customer
service side of things as well, so I offered to let her sit in on a few of my
calls so she could see how I handled tricky situations. She took note of
what I did and then tried it out while I monitored her, giving her some
pointers and a few more suggestions. She seemed really grateful for the
opportunity and improved straight away. Now she's one of our most
successful reps, so I'm very happy I took the time to show her the ropes.*

69. How have you ensured maximum value for money when managing resources?

*The Real Question: Money is tight. Do you know how to squeeze
a pound for all it's worth?*

Top-line Tactic: *Don't shy away from giving them figures.*

For all competency-based questions, providing quantifiable
results is always a good idea, but for questions like this that
are designed to gauge your ability to manage scarce resources,
work within budgetary constraints and make cost savings,
getting down to exact figures is even more important than
usual.

It's also important to keep in mind that, while controlling
the budget is generally a management-level skill, this question might be asked of candidates on any rung of the career
ladder. Companies want people at all levels of the organization to make the most out of company resources. You might

not be setting the budget, but no matter what you do you make choices about using your employer's resources.

The bottom line: don't say this isn't your area, try to choose an example where you can quantify the end result of your efforts and then just apply the STAR method, stressing, as always, not just what you accomplished but the skills and behaviours that got you there. For a more junior-level position, that might sound something like this:

While I wasn't directly charged with handling my department's budget, I'm the type who always likes to get the most for my money, so when my supervisor sent me to pick up some materials we'd had printed I couldn't help being surprised by the size of the bill. At university I was active in the drama club and got flyers and programmes printed up, so I knew we were paying too much. I asked for quotes from a few printers and found one who was 20 per cent cheaper. My supervisor was delighted. We switched suppliers and saved over £5,000 a year.

70. Name some top opinion influencers in this industry

The Real Question: Do you care about thought leadership? Do you agree with the people I agree with?

Top-line Tactic: Get a spread of names, from 'safe hands' to mavericks.

This is one question where a highly motivated career-switcher can score just as well as an industry veteran, because finding opinion influencers has never been easier. The world is positively dripping with industry opinion. Here are two ways of putting together an impressive roster of names.

Power lists: most trade magazines publish an annual survey of the most powerful, influential or just plain wealthy people in a given industry. They usually give these lists corny names like 'Landscape Gardening's Power 100'. Follow the top few names in these lists and you won't go too far wrong. In all probability you'll only be reciting the same old names as everyone else, and maybe the same old ideas too – but you need to start with the classics, as Liberace used to say.

Event speakers: most industries have big trade shows, like the Geneva Motor Show or the Ideal Home Show. These exhibitions usually feature a seminar programme, and the speakers come in two varieties: a keynote speaker and a Sideshow Bob. The keynote speakers are typically on the 'Power 100' lists mentioned above, so you've already got those covered – it's Sideshow Bob you're really interested in. He or she is someone who has yet to make it to the keynote stage but often has the most fresh and radical ideas. You don't have to parrot what they say – they might be on the fringe for a reason – but in interview it's enough to show you're aware of thinkers who exist outside of the consensus. It's also important to show *how* you feed your mind, not just *what* you feed it.

In property, you can't ignore the opinion of people like Donald Trump. In the UK we've got the Candy Brothers or Jon Hunt, who used to be at Foxtons. Their opinions are often influential partly because they get so much exposure anyway. What they say often ends up being true just because they've said it. That's not to take anything away from them – they're prominent because they know what they're talking about, after all.

But I also try to take in the views of people on the fringes, people like Campbell Robb of Shelter. I read his thoughts on the recent sharp rise in house prices we've seen across the UK, when he said homelessness, house prices and our benefit bill will continue to rise out of control if nothing changes. I can't say that he's right, but most people in the industry have vested interests in keeping the whole thing going, and he doesn't – so you can at least be sure he believes what he's saying.

I think the range of opinion in the industry is one of the things I like most about it – I try to read the Property Gazette *every week and I have a few blogs set up as subscriptions.*

That's how I follow opinion leaders.

And if you don't read the trade press every week, be aware you'll almost certainly be competing with people who do.

71. Most people are good at managing up or down, but usually not both. Which one are you?

The Real Question: Are you more charm than substance?

Top-line Tactic: *Try to avoid the distinction by framing 'managing up' and 'managing down' as different skills for different times and then focusing on which you've excelled at . . . so far.*

If you're not familiar with the term, 'managing up' basically means massaging your relationship with your supervisor to keep your work on his or her radar, get access to the resources you need and temper any unrealistic expectations. For some people, it has a pretty nasty connotation of sycophancy and self-promotion.

'I put people into two different categories: people who manage up really well and people who manage down really well, and I love the latter,' Kim Bowers, CEO of CST Brands

183

(a large US company that runs convenience stores), once said in interview, for example. 'It's the folks who manage up really well but have this underlying storm all the time who concern me because you don't know if they're just trying to charm to cover up.'

Other people view 'managing up' as simply good business practice. This difference of opinion, along with the either/or framing of this question, can make it a particularly dangerous one. One way to avoid the obvious pitfalls here is to frame the skills of 'managing up' and 'managing down' as appropriate for different circumstances rather than a fundamental personality divide that you could accidentally end up on the wrong side of.

For me, managing up and managing down are skills I've had to master at different stages in my career based on different situations I've encountered. In my first job after university, for instance, my boss was always travelling and I realized she was sometimes out of the loop on what different team members were working on and we had to wait for her to catch up before we could move on. By sending her progress reports every week and asking specifically about the priorities for the week to come I was able to keep things moving forward. In that case, managing up got me promoted to team leader the following year. Now, I'm working on my skills at managing down.

Another approach for avoiding the either/or framing of the question is to bring up any 360-degree reviews you have been involved in. As these sorts of exercises evaluate your ability to manage up, down and sideways, noting positive reviews is a good way to avoid having to signal allegiance for only team 'managing up' or team 'managing down', as well as stressing your flexibility in communicating well with people no matter their position in the office pecking order.

72. Which websites do you use personally? Why?

The Real Question: Do you keep abreast of industry news? Are you tech savvy?

Top-line Tactic: *Determine what level of technical competence the interviewer is probably looking for and respond appropriately.*

The import of this question very much depends on what sort of job you're applying for. If it's a traditional role in a non-tech company, the chances are the interviewer is fishing mainly to find out if and how you keep abreast of news and industry trends. Possibly, they're also looking for basic tech skills, especially if you suspect they don't possess such skills themselves.

In this case, simply tell the interviewer how you follow developments in the sector, keep up to date with current events and stay in touch with friends and colleagues online. Nothing fancy is required; just make sure you mention the touchstones in your industry. Perhaps that's the *FT* if you're in finance, popular design blogs if you're a designer or LinkedIn if you're a salesperson or recruiter – demonstrate you are familiar with what people in your niche are using and throw in a few personal favourites like that classic car site you're addicted to or your love of Pinterest to give a glimpse of your character. A classic canned answer for this question is to say you use the BBC News website, but most employers have heard this answer so many times that it literally goes without saying. One stated that people 'drink water and read the BBC News website', so try to show a bit of personality in answering this question.

If your prospective employer is a modern, go-ahead inno-vator, on the other hand, the websites you visit and the tech tools you utilize will say a lot more about you. This is like a higher-tech version of school, where your taste in music or fashion choices were a sort of shorthand for your character, but rather than looking at your Dr Martens or popped collar, the question is whether you're a Hotmail or Gmail user, a Firefox or Internet Explorer fan. ('If you're still using an . . .@aol.com email address in 2014 it shows that you can't be bothered to shop around,' declares the *Telegraph*'s Deputy Head of Technology, for example.)

You should have a fair sense of whether this is the sort of industry you work in, and if you get the impression that your interviewer is inviting you to show off your geek credentials, definitely oblige him. Give him the rundown of apps on your iPhone home screen, drop your impressive number of Twitter followers into the conversation, detail how you decided on your preferred blogging platform, walk him through the con-tent of your RSS feed, or complain about how your favourite plugins perform on one browser or another. Either you have no idea what all that means or you do. Whichever camp you're in, go with it.

73. How does your personal social media presence affect your employer?

The Real Question: Are your shenanigans on Facebook or other social media going to embarrass the company?

Top-line Tactic: *Reassure the interviewer that this is the last time they'll ever be discussing your social media presence with you. (There are some exceptions, noted below.)*

For the vast majority of jobs your employer wants to hear exactly nothing about your social media presence. If they already know about it, generally that's because it causes controversy or gossip (or worse yet earns the company some less than excellent publicity), which are really bad outcomes for you.

Most of the time the point of these questions is simply to have you reassure the interviewer that there is nothing salacious or embarrassing to be found on your Facebook or Twitter page, and that you're not about to publicly complain about customers or reveal company secrets.

Frankly, though, these questions are often just red herrings. It's entirely likely that if your pages are public, your interviewer will have already checked them out. Many surveys have been conducted into the extent of this practice. Their results vary, as you'd expect, but the overall trend is clear: roughly one in two firms admit to investigating you online before interview. For this reason, now is a good time to reconsider your privacy settings and comb your profiles to see what sort of image you're projecting to a curious employer. Boozy pics definitely need to go.

There are several exceptions to the less-is-more rule of social media, however. The most obvious is if you are a social media professional, such as a community manager. Then, clearly, your personal social media presence is part of your portfolio and should reflect your skills and values, as well as showcasing your adorable cat or enthusiasm for cupcakes.

The second exception is if you are applying for a role where your high profile as an opinion-shaper would benefit your employer. For instance, if you are a journalist, a large Twitter following could help you locate sources and publicize your work (and also testifies to your ability to capture the public's interest). Public relations pros have a similar relationship to social media. If you're an academic, a reputation as an expert is nearly as important for advancement as your actual expertise, so showing that your blog is the go-to destination for commentary in your field is going to help your candidacy.

Even professionals in less publicity-obsessed fields – real estate or sales, say – can benefit from a strong reputation as an expert on social media if it leads to more referrals or esteem for your employer.

If you can show that your social media presence is a definitive bonus in the specific role you're applying for then by all means go ahead and highlight it. Otherwise, the right answer to these questions is something brief and relatively light-hearted along the lines of:

I never post comments about my work, so no one's interested in my Facebook page except my friends and family. I do enjoy mountain biking, though, and I sometimes rave about how good a route I've discovered is, which can spark off a bit of a debate when someone disagrees with me. It's all in good spirit, though.

74. How have you improved in the last year?

The Real Question: Are you willing to be challenged and learn from mistakes?

Top-line Tactic: *Show that you're always looking to improve.*

Interviewees often tie themselves in knots trying to cover up past weaknesses and mistakes. As we discussed when we looked at questions like *What are your greatest weaknesses?*, this is a mistake. Employers aren't mad. They know that no one is perfect and all of us – or at least the most valuable – experience setbacks and learn from them.

This question isn't necessarily a 'gotcha!' designed to trick you into revealing imperfections; it's a test of your self-knowledge, resilience and ability to improve in areas where you're less strong. Therefore, your answer should aim to convince the interviewer you're happy to accept a challenge and learn from the experience – paint yourself as the type of person who is always looking to grow and improve. It's fine if that involves making some mistakes along the way.

Employers love goal-oriented applicants because an interest in setting targets indicates just this sort of growth mentality. So when you discuss improvements, make sure that after you outline an area where you were in need of development, you mention that you explicitly set a goal for yourself. Don't skip this step! Wrap up the story with you triumphantly meeting that goal. Language like, *My New Year's resolution was . . .* or *After my last annual review I decided . . .* can help.

What sorts of improvement impress employers? Both professional and personal goals you have met can work, as those who tend to strive for self-betterment at home do so at the office as well. Consider whether any of these apply to you:

- Training courses you've completed.
- Increasingly positive reviews with manager, peers or customers.
- Explicit targets you set and improved upon (like sales quotas, customer service response times, or work quantity).
- Innovative strategies you've tried at work – just make sure you can pinpoint the results.
- Moments of self-assessment that led to personal improvement.

75. Tell me about a time a client was especially unhappy and what you did to resolve the situation

The Real Question: Can you handle conflict in a professional manner?

Top-line Tactic: *Put away the blame and the boxing gloves. Instead, focus on a time you took responsibility and calmly resolved a conflict.*

Can clients be unreasonable? Sure, but this isn't the time to delve into all the varieties of unreasonable you've come across in the course of your career. The interviewer isn't looking to trade war stories; rather, the intention is to assess whether your reaction to conflict is constructive and professional.

To answer this question well, you'll need to display basic good character. Empathizing when others get heated is a hard but essential business skill, as is the ability to take responsibility for problems. When you're wracking your brain for a story for this one, don't choose an incident when you made an egregious mistake, but do select a situation where you had the opportunity to be the bigger person – even if that means accepting the blame for the conflict.

As always when applying the STAR method, make sure you're actively resolving the situation yourself. Never tell a story that ends with you handing the issue off to a higher authority. Never blame a client or co-worker.

When I was assistant manager at my local leisure centre, a woman came in very upset, demanding a refund for her daughter's swimming lessons. I could see the counter assistant was getting flustered, so I stepped in and calmly asked the woman what was wrong. Apparently, after several lessons her daughter was still terrified of the water. I apologized that her little girl hadn't made any progress, and said I could see why she was disappointed. It was against our policy to offer refunds – although, to be honest, I think it's better to have a satisfied customer, anyway – so I explained that children respond differently to different teaching styles and offered to switch her daughter to another class. She agreed to that, and after a week I saw her again and she said her daughter loved her new teacher and was going great guns. In fact, she signed her up for the next set of lessons then and there.

Despite the old saying, the fact is the customer isn't always right (though most companies like to let them think they are). You shouldn't appear as if you'll concede to every unreasonable demand, but you do want to demonstrate that you can stay cool and work towards a constructive solution.

76. Tell me about a time you made an important decision in the absence of a manager. Why did you reach that decision?

The Real Question: Can you think independently or do you need constant handholding?

Top-line Tactic: *Convince the interviewer that you can be trusted to make good calls without supervision.*

The good news with this question is, should you get the job, your new boss probably won't be a micro-manager. If the interviewer is asking about independent decision making, that's a good clue that the role will involve working under your own steam and thinking through tough calls logically without lots of support.

You need to show that you have a level-headed, logical approach to decision making and aren't paralysed by responsibility. Make sure you apply the STAR approach to a real-life example of a time you made a stellar independent call. Provide plenty of detail about how you reached your conclusion in order to demonstrate that you have the ability to make similarly good decisions in your new role. Show that you can discern truly momentous decisions that require calling in reinforcements.

As parts-supply manager I was responsible for fulfilling client orders. If there was any deviation from normal procedure, such as a discount or an express delivery, it generally had to be approved by the floor manager. But he was away when I got a call from one of our best customers in a panic, who were working on a rush job and had accidentally under-ordered and needed a delivery that afternoon. I said we'd do our best and I'd get straight back to them.

I'd worked there long enough to know what the floor manager would have done, so I felt confident to make the decision myself. I followed the usual procedure, which was to check the size and status of the customer's account and ask the transport department if we could make the delivery. The account was a good one, and one of our drivers would be in the area and was willing to do some overtime, so I rang back and said we could get them the parts if they'd agree to a small rush-delivery fee. They were happy, the driver was happy, and so was my boss, who said I'd made the right call. I think the way I handled that situation was one of the reasons I was promoted to floor manager at a different branch a few months later.

77. Can you tell me about a recent situation where you took the initiative and made something happen?

The Real Question: Are you a go-getter or will you wait to be assigned tasks?

Top-line Tactic: *Demonstrate you can identify problems, not just solve those that are handed to you.*

For employers, team members who will go above and beyond their job description are pure gold. It isn't all that difficult to find people who will competently execute the work they're tasked with. But someone who will identify problems proactively and find creative ways to solve them is rare – and incredibly valuable.

So while this question is fairly straightforward, it is important to nail your answer. As ever with 'tell me about' questions, apply the trusty STAR method to paint a picture for the interviewer of a time you went outside your job description to improve something for your employer. Don't just tell them you're willing to take the initiative – show them you've already done so to great effect.

When I started at my last company, there was no proper induction process. If I had a question there was nowhere specific I could go for information. I had to ask round everybody, trying to find what I was after, which wasted a lot of time both for me and for them and meant getting myself up to speed took longer than it should have.

So when I was settled in, I decided to collect all the information I had rounded up from various sources and create a training document for newcomers to the department. I laid out key processes step by step so even a complete novice could follow them and then asked whether I'd left anything out. My colleagues made several great suggestions, which I incorporated before presenting the finished article to my boss. She was really pleased with the initiative, and new people now get stuck into their jobs within a week, which must be both good for them and save the company money.

78. What is the biggest issue between you and your current/previous manager?

The Real Question: Can you take criticism? Can you be flexible in order to fit in?

Top-line Tactic: *Present yourself as coachable.*

This is a tough one and the phrasing makes it even tougher. If the question was *Tell me about your relationship with your previous boss*, no doubt you could rattle off a positive answer straight away, but how do you respond when the interviewer is specifically asking for problems, and problems *with you personally*?

Here's what you definitely shouldn't do: don't go negative on your boss, no matter how tempting that might be. Not only does the interviewer not really care about your boss (he's thinking of hiring you, not them, after all), but complaining that any interpersonal issues were someone else's fault will just make you look nasty, untrustworthy and unwilling to take responsibility.

The only way you can come out of this question looking good is to present a problem your boss had with you as a coachable moment you seized as an opportunity for improvement. As with previous questions, moderate flaws are fine and show growth potential – as long as they've been corrected on another company's time. Just make sure you don't pick something that's an issue of character or that's fundamental to your ability to do the job (engineers can't be sloppy about calculations; sales people shouldn't admit to disliking social interaction, etc.).

When I first started, we didn't see eye to eye about communicating work progress at all. I was anxious to make a good impression and determined to be as productive as possible, and I thought writing status updates was a distraction and not the best use of my time so I decided not to write them. My boss explained that she needed more information about the progress of my work both to make sure there were no bottlenecks in the workflow, and also because senior management were pressing her for the information. I hadn't really thought about it from her perspective before, but once we'd talked it through I could see I was being a bit selfish. Now I make sure I send her a weekly update. I also suggested a spreadsheet where we could check off each stage of order processing that would show not only my progress, but also the flow of work across the whole team. After that, we got on much better. The experience definitely taught me the value of communicating my work clearly to my colleagues.

79. What is your favourite product/service in the industry?

The Real Question: How familiar are you with this industry? Do you understand what makes a good product and can you persuasively express your preferences?

Top-line Tactic: *The product you choose doesn't matter; the coherence of your thoughts on it are what counts.*

Just as companies want you to be familiar with the organization's mission, products and culture when applying, they also want you to know something about the industry in general. They're out to best the competition, after all. How are you going to help them do that if you're clueless about your rivals and haven't thought about what makes for a good product in the category?

As is the case with many interview questions, what you choose to talk about is less important than *how* you talk about it, though one of the worst possible outcomes is to be stumped when asked about your favourite products. This is definitely one you want to think about in advance.

To ace this question, simply tell the interviewer your choice and lay out the reasons for selecting that product, focusing less on your personal preferences and more on why you think this product was a great move for the business that created it. No one cares that you love a particular feature. What they want to know is that you understand what factors made the product a success. A few terms from product management can help you think about what exactly makes this product stand out:

- **Purpose:** What problem does the product solve?
- **Growth:** How did that product hook you? Have you recommended it to other people?
- **Engagement:** How often do you use the product? Why do you go back so often?
- **Trade-offs:** No product is perfect. In which areas does this product excel and which does it choose not to emphasize? Why is the balance this product strikes better than other possible ways of approaching things?
- **Competition:** A product is rarely unique. What's so good about this one compared to others on the market?

- **Staying power:** Why are you loyal to the product? How long will this continue?

Put those together and you might get an answer that sounds something like this:

When it comes to consumer goods, I'm really impressed with M— cleaning products. I think consumer interest in green options is exploding and they do a great job tapping into that. Plus, the claim that you could literally eat their products if you wanted is really memorable – when I recommend M— to friends I always mention that and it sticks in their minds. Of course, some people might argue that makes it sound like the products might not be as effective, but I think the surprise value of the claim outweighs that worry. Especially as once you try them you see that they really work.

If you are applying for a product management position this question will probably play a far more central role in your interview than if you're up for a job in something like finance or manufacturing. In that case, your ability to be persuasive about trade-offs, as well as your ability to pinpoint possible improvements for products that are already great will be more highly prized. Those applying for a product management role should prepare for push back – the interviewer wants to see if you can stand up to opposing opinions and make a convincing case for your point of view.

80. What is 10 per cent of 100?

The Real Question: Exactly what it says on the tin: can you do basic maths?

Top-line Tactic: *No fancy stuff required. Just answer.*

You hardly need a book on interviewing to tell you that 10 per cent of 100 is 10, so why include such a straightforward question here? Simply to tip you off that these sorts of questions might be coming. They're particularly common at interviews for retail positions, when you might be asked, for instance, to calculate the discount on an item of a particular price or mentally work out the correct change. School maths class should have equipped you with all you need to know to nail these sorts of questions, but here are a few tricks to bear in mind:

- If they're asking for a more difficult percentage, say 8 per cent of 40, the fastest way to work it out in the heat of an interview is to calculate 1 per cent of 40 (namely 40 divided by 100 = 0.4) then multiply that by 8 to get 3.2.
- You can also add smaller percentages together to reach your answer. Finding 10 per cent and 1 per cent can often help with working out less straightforward questions. For example, *What is 18 per cent of 40?*

> 18 per cent of 40 = 10 per cent + 8 per cent
> 10 per cent = 4; 1 per cent = 0.4
> 8 per cent = 3.2 (as above)
> 18 per cent of 40 = 4 + 3.2 = 7.2.

- If you're asked to work out the amount of change due to a customer, count up from the total cost of the sale to the amount of cash you receive (in your head or out loud). For example, if the total comes to £37.14 and the customer hands you £40:

  6p takes you to £37.20
  another 80p takes you to £38
  another £2 takes you to £40
  and hey presto you have your answer: £2.86.

- Algebra can come in handy from time to time, too. Another question I heard recently asked a candidate to imagine that a company's sales figures doubled one year and then doubled again the next. By what total percentage did sales increase over the two years?

  Call original sales x.
  This figure doubled is $2x$; doubling again makes $4x$.
  $4x - x = 3x$
  The total percentage increase in sales is therefore 300 per cent.

Alternatively, ask them if you can use whatever tools you're expected to use in the job, then take out your calculator!

81. Tell me about a time you supported a member of your team who was struggling

The Real Question: Can you balance the needs of your team with the organization's objectives?

Top-line Tactic: *Show them you can be warm and fuzzy in pursuit of the bottom line.*

This might seem like a pretty straightforward competency-based question, but there is actually one big hidden consideration to think about when selecting which story you're going to apply the STAR method to. While a great many companies value teamwork, emotional intelligence and empathy in their people, the cold, hard truth is they do so because they think that helping and caring is of benefit to their bottom line.

The best answers stress that not only did you support a teammate, but that your support translated into higher performance for the company. You want to show that you're nice ... in a way that improved productivity. For recent grads, a good answer might look something like this:

At university, I was in put charge of six students who were working on a field project. A large part of the work was information gathering, so attending the clinic where we were volunteering in order to collect data was obviously really important. One lad kept missing his assigned days, which meant more work for everyone else.

I took him for a coffee, brought up the fact that he had been missing meetings and asked what was wrong. He explained that he was snowed under with work from another class he was taking and was struggling to fit in his commitment to our project. I had taken the class myself and knew how hard it was, but I also knew there was tutoring available to help students who were having a rough time. I put him in touch with the tutoring centre and his attendance at the project quickly improved, which nipped any resentment within the group in the bud and ensured we'd have all the data we'd need for the final analysis. The project ended up getting high marks, and the student passed his class as well.

Those further along in their careers might think about times they engaged in mentoring (or paired up employees who could coach or support each other), endeavoured to help colleagues get up to speed with new technology or processes, provided training or workshops to fill skills gaps, or offered compassionate leave to colleagues struggling with personal matters.

82. In your current job, how many hours a week must you work to get it all done?

The Real Question: Are you flexible? Do you have many outside commitments?

Top-line Tactics: *If you have outside commitments, mention them now. If you can be flexible, say you will be flexible.*

An ambiguous question if ever there was. There are at least three interpretations:

1. The interviewer might be sneakily asking if you have dependants or an all-encompassing hobby, either of which might cause you to rush out the door at 4 p.m.
2. They might hope to establish whether you track your time

efficiently. If you're the sort of person who knows exactly how long it takes to get a job done, you're probably blessed with above-average organizational skills.

3. They could be asking to see if you'll pitch in when the job calls for long hours, or whether you walk out at the same time each day on principle.

In many ways it doesn't matter why they're asking, because, for them and you, the ideal answer is the 100 per cent honest answer. If you have dependants, there's no point denying it. If you're the sort of person who makes a sharp division between work and the rest of your life, such that you work your contracted hours only, then there's no point denying that either. It's better to say so now, because, rightly or wrongly, there is a cultural assumption among employers that team members will chip in 'as and when' (in fact it's a common term in the contract). If that's not you, they need to know.

If you're like most people then you probably are prepared to work long hours but you probably also don't keep a running total of hours worked. If so, your answer to this question should, for dignity's sake, make clear that you're someone who values their time.

I've never tracked my hours because it's never been something I've worried about. Sometimes you have to work long hours, which is fine by me. Obviously, I have a life outside of work too, but I'm sure there's room for both. Do you have a company policy on the issue?

If nothing else, they probably won't be expecting you to answer this question with another question. That's often a risky tactic, but here it's OK as your answer has given them a little of what they came for, namely a sense that you'll chip in.

83. Give an example of a time you've had to improvise to achieve your goal

The Real Question: Can you think on your feet?

Top-line Tactic: *Combine the best tactics for answering both curveballs and competency-based questions.*

This question is actually an unholy mash-up of a curveball and a competency-based question. Like other curveballs, it's designed to knock you off your game by probing how you handle something you haven't prepared for. Like a competency-based question, it asks for an anecdote from your past professional experience.

So what sort of anecdote are you looking for? Improvisation is all about facing the chaos, trusting yourself to handle the unexpected, and overcoming fear of failure, to act. Find a real situation in your working life when the universe threw up a surprise challenge and you handled it with the cleverness (and sense of humour) of a stand-up comic or the grace of a jazz musician. For example:

My previous company hosted two client conferences a year, which were an important revenue driver for the business and a vital source of leads for our secondary consulting business. For each event we booked an MC to introduce speakers and keep things entertaining. Last year at our autumn conference, our scheduled MC came down with food poisoning the night before the event. It was too late to find a replacement, so as the event manager I had to fill in.

I have to admit I'm the sort who is far more comfortable handling the backstage stuff than getting up in front of several hundred important clients, but I had to do something. I had a huddle with my team and we came up with several great ideas on how to keep up the energy in the room – icebreaker activities and so on – and we also prepped index cards with the speaker details. I was a bit of a nervous wreck that morning, but I got up and told the crowd what had happened and that they were stuck with me. They were actually really supportive – I think everyone has been outside their comfort zone occasionally and people respect your willingness to have a go. Thanks to the last-minute prep and some deep breathing, I managed to get through it, and I even had great feedback from our audience questionnaires. Also, I'm much less afraid of public speaking now, which is a bonus.

To give an example from real life, a Reed advisor once lent his suit to an unemployed job seeker to attend an interview. How could we not employ someone prepared to do that?

SIX

CURVEBALL AND CREATIVITY QUESTIONS

There is some overlap between these two categories, which is why I've combined them into what is a colourful group of questions. Interviewers ask them for a variety of reasons and, dare I say it, one of those reasons might be to have a bit of fun. There are infinite permutations and variations of the questions I've included here, but the following pages will help you when you find yourself at an interview feeling stressed, confused – or just thinking *What?*

Curveball questions

There are two types of curveball question: the useful and the illegal.

A useful curveball question might be: *Every CV has at least one lie in it. What's yours?*

It is of course designed to put you under pressure, because, as the late Bobby Womack sang in 'Across 110th Street', you don't know what you'll do *until* you're put under pressure. Nobody knows – certainly not your interviewer, to whom you are most likely a complete stranger.

Not even the best candidates should hope to get through

an interview without being totally stumped at least once, and when it happens to you, don't assume there's nothing left to play for. Your interviewer is not necessarily looking for a right answer: instead they're looking for you to go down in flames with a certain degree of élan.

As for illegal curveball questions, such as your plans for a family, I can only hope that you are never asked any. Most interviewers are fair and decent people with enough sense to know that they're just as much on show as you are. Nevertheless, illegal questions have not disappeared just because they're illegal, so later on we'll prep you with a few ways to defend yourself.

Creativity questions

Among the incredibly popular series of TED lectures on YouTube, Sir Ken Robinson's 2007 lecture (*How Schools Kill Creativity*) is the most-viewed of them all – no mean feat, given the standard of the competition. Sir Ken's speech touched a chord in millions of people all over the world, presumably many of whom feel school throttled *their* creativity. Although I don't necessarily agree with everything Sir Ken says, I certainly agree with him when he says:

A child starting school in 2007 will be retiring in 2065. But nobody has a clue, despite all the expertise that's been on parade [at TED] what the world will look like in *five years'* time. And yet we're meant to be educating them for [2065]. The unpredictability is extraordinary.

Many of the jobs that Reed will be dealing with in ten years' time haven't been invented yet. They don't have a name, a salary, a typical career path or a person specification. The world will discover these new jobs only to the extent that creatively gifted people can find space to invent them, using the dazzling array of new technologies now unfurling around us. Creativity, therefore, is no longer an asset only to the so-called 'creative industries' – it is now a must-have attribute in every industry.

That's why employers are increasingly keen for you to establish your creative credentials. Often, they'll want you to be creative *on the spot*, such as by asking offbeat and out-wardly useless questions like *If you could be any type of biscuit, which would it be?* Impersonating a biscuit won't change the world, but the sort of person who can riff and improvise around abstract subjects just might.

If you find this kind of question to be a terrifying prospect, you can calm yourself with the thought that there is no one right way to answer it – divergent answers are OK. It does help to familiarize yourself with a wide variety of creativity questions.

But although it's useful to go over some of the different categories of question, it's important to remember that the only thing that will really count for much are your answers to individual questions. That, plus your personal reaction to the interviewer sitting in front of you.

There is clearly an overlap between curveball and creativity questions. A question like *What kind of superhero would you be?* can be deployed both to allow you to show your creativity and to put some pressure on you as a curveball. Rather than split hairs, I have put all such questions into this chapter.

84. If you were an animal what would you be?

The Real Question: How do you respond when you haven't had the chance to rehearse an answer?

Top-line Tactic: *Don't let the weirdness throw you. Roll with the punches and have fun – there are very few wrong answers.*

There are tons of variations on this sort of question, from *If you could be any superhero, which one would you be?* to *What colour are you?* They're all designed to do the same thing: rattle you out of simply reciting the canned answers you have prepared for the interview and get you to reveal who you really are under that polished exterior. According to some interviewers, this sort of curveball question is also a good way to test your ability to think on your feet. If a company values a sense of humour in a team member, this might also be a good way to judge that.

As Mo Jan, founder of Webalytix, told the *Financial Times*: 'I use curveball questions for the simple purpose of seeing how quickly potential candidates can respond – whether they can respond succinctly and with a good sense of humour. It's not so much getting the answer right but more importantly demonstrating that they are able to take it in the right spirit and see how creative they can be on the spot.'

Which brings us to the first, most important point about answering these questions: there is no right answer. The interviewer isn't looking to hire only those who identify as Superman, a giraffe or pale chartreuse. So relax, the only way you can go wrong is to clam up, get uncomfortable or mumble something barely intelligible. The interviewer wants to see your personality, so show it to them. If you have to hide it eight hours a day for the next several years, you're going to end up pretty miserable anyway!

Which isn't to say there aren't better and worse answers to this type of question. The best ones somehow manage to highlight a quality of the animal (or superhero, etc.) that lines up with the skills needed for the job you're applying for. Here's a great example from HootSuite CEO Ryan Holmes, who asked a very similar question of his assistant when she was interviewing and got an outstanding answer:

During her interview I asked my current Executive Assistant what was her favourite animal. She told me it was a duck, because ducks are calm on the surface and hustling like crazy getting things done under the surface.

I think this was an amazing response and a perfect description for the role of an EA. For the record, she's been working with us for over a year now and is amazing at her job.

You're unlikely to think of something this clever straight away, so if you're faced with an off-the-wall question like this, feel free to take a long pause to consider. You can even say, 'Give me a moment to think about this one.' You might even think about getting into the spirit of fun and honest disclosure by asking the same question right back to the interviewer.

85. Every CV has at least one lie in it. What's yours?

The Real Question: Are there any untruths lurking in your CV?

Top-line Tactic: *Avoid the question as asked. Of course there aren't any lies in your CV . . .*

There's no doubt about it, this is a stinger, but unfortunately there is a good reason employers would ask it. One recent survey found that as many as 20 per cent of job seekers admitted they're prepared to lie on their CVs.

Hopefully though, you're not one of them, as not only is lying catastrophic for your chances of getting the job if it's discovered, it's also a sure-fire way to end up with a job you're poorly prepared to handle. Which makes this one of the rare occasions when you want to try to avoid the question as asked.

CVs are an art form and while outright untruths are a terrible idea, presenting your accomplishments in the best possible light is the whole point of the exercise. But when the interviewer asks this question, it isn't the time to discuss the salesmanship of CV writing. It is the time to try to pass this off with a joke or, should your wit fail you, even a flat denial. Try something like:

Well, it says under hobbies there that I enjoy keeping fit. My wife would say that's stretching the truth! Seriously though, I don't believe there are any lies on my CV. I believe integrity on the job is very important and that starts with your CV.

86. Have you ever been fired?

The Real Question: Would getting fired explain the gap on your CV? Might history repeat itself?

Top-line Tactic: *Be upfront and show what's changed.*

You got fired? Welcome to one of the world's biggest clubs.

It's not a particularly exclusive club, but it does have some very famous members, some of whom joined for reasons you might find surprising:

- Steve Jobs was once fired for making computers that, at the time, only a few people wanted.
- Walt Disney was once sacked from a newspaper for his 'lack of creativity'.
- Elvis Presley got the boot from the Nashville Grand Ole Opry for being bad at singing.
- Thomas Edison got canned for being sloppy in a laboratory.
- While working as a TV news reporter, Oprah Winfrey was shown the door for being 'too emotionally connected to her audience'.

You get the idea: the right person in the right job, but somehow at the wrong time. It can happen to anyone.

But before you go comparing yourself to Steve Jobs in front of your future boss, remember that the main point of an interview is to determine whether you and the job are a good fit, not to make a long, improvised speech that drags out all the little details and injustices of your firing.

And although it surely hurts to be fired, the interviewer is not there to help you lay your ghosts to rest – you must do that yourself, long before you go interviewing again, or else how will you walk in with your head held high?

So, before you attend an interview, how do you make peace with yourself for getting fired? You should start by assuming your interviewer *knows* you got fired but still invited you for interview (there's a chance they do know – for every industry there's a grapevine). Next, be honest with yourself about why you got fired. If it was somebody else's fault *entirely*, you're probably doing this bit wrong. Then call your old employer and ask what they plan to say about you to prospective employers. This is a daunting but entirely necessary step – and you might even hear that they plan to say nothing negative at all. Regardless of what they say, acknowledge your role in the termination but say that you're looking to make a fresh start. Few bosses would be so stonyhearted as to get in the way of your reform and your call will help to tone down any possible criticism of you they give to the other firm. And mostly, your ex-employer is going to say very little about you anyway, as a matter of policy, whether you were fired or not. Cheer yourself up with that.

So much for before you go for interview. What are you supposed to say on the day? Above all, you should show how you've grown from the experience and you should give them the truth, the whole truth and nothing but the truth. Often, and especially if you've done well at the interview, your interviewer will merely be eager to establish that you got fired for reasons that are unlikely to replicate themselves in your new job. This is why frankness helps.

Don't carp or bring personalities into it – either yours or that of your former boss. If it's remotely plausible, say you enjoyed your time at your ex-company.

They'll expect you to have thought long and hard about why you were fired, and that you learned from it. Many people never get that far, choosing instead to be chippy about it – so put some space between those people and you, by remaining cheerful and optimistic. Describe your firing from the company's point of view. If you think the firing was justified, say so. You'll get extra points if you admit that you would have done the same thing yourself. Mention any good appraisals or results you received in your former employment.

If you got fired for performance issues, or maturity issues, reflect on what you've done to raise your game lately. Some redundancies are made to look like sackings, and if you suspect that happened to you, say so without bitterness or rancour. In countries where firing is legally easier, some firms, especially struggling ones, will fire you in your probation period simply to avoid the possibility of being taken to a tribunal. It's not fair or nice, but it happens, especially to the young. A seasoned interviewer will recognize the phenomenon.

Did you keep customers and other contacts from that time? Show that your departure from the company was not a total loss in terms of what you brought forward.

If you're suing for unfair dismissal, keep it to yourself unless asked. It'll just open up more uncertainty about your character.

Watch your body language: don't be hunched and defensive. Maintain eye contact. To sound less accusatory, use collective pronouns. Say 'we couldn't agree', not 'he disagreed'. Keep it short – if they want more, they'll ask.

Ask if you have addressed their concerns: that's a good way to draw a line under this part of the conversation:

I enjoyed my time at LastCo but I think they were entirely justified to end my employment there. I've had time to think about what happened and, with the benefit of hindsight, I can see a number of things that I should have done differently, and one or two things that I won't be doing again.

I was fired because I didn't make my sales targets after a restructuring of the sales territory. I should have said sooner that I was struggling to do what they wanted of me; maybe I was a bit complacent because I'd done well before, both in that job and at that company, but nothing stays the same and when my circumstances changed I didn't change fast enough. But it was definitely a case of being overwhelmed rather than uninterested. It made me take a long, hard look at how I manage my workload.

I was sorry to leave the job, and I felt a bit let down, but we didn't part on bad terms. To be fair, a lot of good things came from LastCo – I still have most of the sales contacts I made there, and some good friends too. I'm sure LastCo would give me a good reference if you asked them.

I appreciate that you, as an interviewer, have to take a lot of things on trust, but I hope I've put your mind at rest on this point.

87. Tell me about a time you went against company policy

The Real Question: Can you think independently? Are you a troublemaker/whistleblower?

Top-line Tactic: *It's OK to present yourself as an occasional rebel, but make sure you're a rebel with a cause who goes through proper channels.*

Things may be changing slightly in the corporate world, but most companies are still far from democracies. While many tout their commitment to innovation and limited bureaucracy, most continue to value consistency and the ability to conform to 'how things are done around here'. For this reason, you need to handle this question with care.

To impress your interviewer, you'll need to walk the line separating a company yes-man from a disruptive rebel who is difficult to manage. This question is probably designed to sniff out and eliminate both extremes. The key to getting the balance right is to choose a time you disagreed with a company policy not for personal reasons, but because you felt the rule wasn't serving the company's or client's interests.

Rather than confess that you once went rogue or bent the

rules, search for a time when you discovered a company policy that wasn't suitable to the situation and made a compelling business case to change it to your manager. That way you can demonstrate your independence of thought, good grasp of business principles *and* your healthy regard for going through proper channels.

At A&B it was company policy that no one could be promoted until they'd worked there six months. It wasn't something I questioned until I hired a recent grad who was brilliant. Within weeks of him starting I could see he was far too good for the entry-level job he was doing and, given his skills, I doubted we'd be able to hold on to him if I couldn't give him more responsibility. Plus, it just seemed a waste not to utilize him to his full potential.

I told both my supervisor and HR that the company stood to lose a great person because of an arbitrary rule. It turned out that the rule had been made years before, and HR agreed to reconsider. Given the exceptional circumstances, they ended up letting me shift him into a new role straight away. He's still with the company today and one of our highest performers, so that's definitely one time I was happy to have challenged company policy.

It's also worth noting that a job interview is an opportunity for two-way discovery. Of course they're learning about you, but you can also learn plenty about them, including from the questions they ask. If you are a bit of a free spirit, questions like this should send up a red flag for you. They indicate that the company is very keen on structure and compliance, so consider whether this is truly the environment for you.

88. Tell me about your family

The Real Question: My family is important to understanding me, so I'd like to understand you the same way.

Top-line Tactic: Assume innocent intentions (mostly you'll be right to do so).

It has to be said that some interviewers, when faced with a female candidate, ask this question simply to discover if she has children or plans for babies or perhaps elderly dependants – but those are not the only reasons. Some interviewers ask this question for much more benign (and legal) reasons.

First, the question helps to reveal how your relationships work when you've little choice in the matter. Your family is a group of people you don't choose to be with – just like the world of work.

Additionally, some interviewers ask the question because they genuinely want to go some way to accommodating the candidate's family needs, knowing that some candidates have their jobs partly defined for them *by* their family. Being aware of someone's hinterland, and how their work fits into it, is just common sense – some would say it'd be inconsiderate not to ask.

It's also a good way of finding out who and what has been influential in your upbringing. As one of Reed's recruiters put it:

We have a client whose interview process is very, very different. At a candidate's first interview, the interviewer doesn't ask anything related to the job, or anything about key skills. It's all about the candidate's family, their upbringing, and why they're sat in front of them. It's *Tell me about what your mum and dad did when you were little, Tell me why you're sat in front of me now.*

It's a way of seeing who influenced the candidate when they were younger, seeing what kind of career path they choose to go down. It's quite a bizarre way of interviewing but we tell our candidates that that particular client always interviews that way – else they'd be mortified on the day, I think.

Interestingly, that interviewer really got to the bottom of my mum and dad, and why I'm doing recruitment for my career. I can imagine it catching on, actually.

Naturally, it can be hard to work out whether the interviewer is genuinely asking about your background (legal), or your plans for a family (illegal). You've usually nothing but your instinct to guide you. Suffice to say that you should not automatically assume that the interviewer is trying to pull a fast one. To some interviewers, hiring you *is* hiring your family.

89. Are you married? Planning to have kids? When did you start your career? Where are you from originally? Do you celebrate any specific religious holidays?

The Real Question: Will you be distracted by your personal life? Will you fit in around here?

Top-line Tactic: *These questions are illegal. Your response depends on how offensive you find them.*

What employers are allowed to ask about and what they're not is straightforward. Questions about your marital status, sexual orientation, children or intent to have them, religion, age, disability status and country of origin are out of bounds and, technically speaking, interviewers can get slapped with discrimination lawsuits if they ignore these rules. In practice though, some interviewers are ignorant (or sneaky) and will ask anyway. How do you handle these uncomfortable questions?

Sometimes you would be justified in bluntly telling the interviewer their ham-fisted question is completely inappropriate, but if you still want the job after they ask, this will definitely hurt, if not completely destroy, your chances. Other times, an interview is more conversational and you end up wandering into technically dicey territory through the seemingly innocent flow of conversation. If that happens and you're personally not bothered by a question, go ahead and answer.

But what about the middle ground? Legalities aside, interviewers have a genuine interest in your commitment and ability to do the job. Your personal situation does, in reality, sometimes impact that. So how do you respond when you sense the interview is probing off-limits topics but also believe their motivation is not blatantly discriminatory. (Basically, the question is annoying . . . but not annoying enough to make you not want the job.) One good technique in these situations is to address the underlying worry that's behind the question while dodging the specific query:

Q: Do you intend to have kids anytime soon?
A: I plan to keep working whether or not I decide to have a family.

Q: What an interesting accent! Where are you from originally?
A: My family are from [country], *but I've been living in the UK for many years/since I was . . .*

Q: Will you be taking any specific religious holidays?
A: I've never had any issues staying within the limits of my employer's

policy on leave before and don't imagine that will be a problem here either.

One final option is the blatant dodge. The subtext of this response is essentially, 'That's inappropriate and I'm not going to answer,' but the wrapping is warmer and less aggressive.

Q: Do you have kids?

A: (Pointing to a picture on the desk). I see you have two. How old are they?

If the interviewer persists despite your attempts to nudge the conversation back on track you might want to think long and hard about whether this is really the right company for you.

90. Where did you last go on holiday?

The Real Question: Will I like chatting with you around the water cooler every day?

Top-line Tactic: *The only tactic here is to be the most charming version of yourself you can muster.*

Don't be deceived: just because a question isn't hard hitting, doesn't mean it's not important. As we covered in the introductory chapters of this book, interviewers are human and, like the rest of us, they often judge candidates on personality and vague impressions of likeability as much as they do on their assessment of hard skills and competencies.

This question is just small talk, it's true, but small talk can win or lose you the job, so while it's not particularly important whether you went to Malta, Moscow or Morecambe on your last holiday, it is important to use all the tools at your disposal to be charming when the conversation turns to this sort of personal chit-chat. Top tips include:

- **Ask as much as you answer:** People like those who are interested in them, so don't be shy about making this a two-way conversation. *I was just in Rome a couple of months ago. We had the most amazing pizza. Have you ever been to Italy?*
- **Don't be a robot:** Books like this can sometimes make answering job interview questions sound a bit mechanical – they ask X, you say Y, move on to the next topic – but good small talk is free flowing, so don't be afraid to go off on a tangent when the conversation turns to more personal topics. *You went fly fishing? Funnily enough I tried fly fishing just last summer in Scotland. It was an amazing time but I was terrible at it. How long did it take you to master?*
- **Pay attention to body language:** Body language is particularly important in the context of small talk, where the main point is personal style and charm. Make eye contact (if you find this hard, focus on the bridge of their nose and you'll look like you're looking directly into their eyes, but you won't feel like you're staring them out). Don't fidget – it will convey impatience. Smile.
- **Avoid anything controversial:** If your last trip reveals something about your outside interests that you're not comfortable discussing or worry might not be something the interviewer can relate to (a planning weekend with your activist group, a religious retreat, a rather wild hen weekend that doesn't paint you in the most professional light) go ahead and mention the trip before that. Also avoid embarrassing tales of getting epically lost, forgetting your passport, or any other reminiscence that could paint you in a bad light.

91. Tell me about the last good idea you had

The Real Question: How innovative are you?

Top-line Tactic: *Take the open-ended nature of this question as an invitation to highlight something about your skills you've been dying to cover.*

Your first impulse may be to view the open-ended nature of this question as a curse, but it's actually a blessing. Before you go into an interview you should have a good idea of what you want the interviewer to know about you by the end of the discussion. No doubt you've seen politicians do something similar in interviews – they always have a point they want to get across and are very skilled at answering questions to suit their own agenda.

But just as politicians can take this too far, job candidates can also overplay this strategy by sticking religiously to their preset plan and failing to genuinely listen to and respond to the interviewer. Because of its open-ended nature, this question is a great opportunity to slip in one of your talking points without seeming like a parrot. Take this question as your cue to tell the interviewer something that you don't want to leave the interview room without sharing.

That being said, those key points you're dying to get across shouldn't just be about you. They need to be tailored to each specific role. Sometimes it is even the case that the interviewer has a list of criteria that you need to meet in order to match the job specifications.

Non-work examples are a possibility, but make sure they tie back to a character trait or skill that is relevant for the job at hand. No one cares about the brilliant idea you had for your last dance recital unless you can demonstrate that you'll bring the same creativity to bear in your new role. Be particularly cautious about giving a personal example if the interviewer's previous questions have given you the sense there is any concern about your motivation or commitment to the job. If there's already a suspicion that you are going to be watching the clock for the second it hits 5 p.m., then talking about your passion for dance is going to come across as a glaring warning sign that your true priorities lie outside the office.

92. Would you mind if I approached your former/current employer for a reference?

The Real Question: Do you have anything to hide?

Top-line Tactic: *Reference checks should be no problem, but if you require discretion when dealing with your current employer, it's fine to ask for it.*

An interviewer asking if it's OK to check your references isn't a sure-fire sign the job is yours, but it's a pretty good signal that they're at least interested. So be encouraged if you hear this question.

The content of the references you provide should never be in doubt, so you should have no hesitations about a hiring manager speaking to any of the contacts you provide. Only offer up the names of people who will speak well of you, preferably your current or previous supervisors. However, in certain situations the timing of reference checks may be somewhat tricky.

Previous employers ought to be no problem. It's a good

idea to check with them to ask if they mind providing a reference and to give them a heads-up that they might receive a call. If you haven't taken care of this before the interview, it's fine to get in touch after and let them know someone might be checking up on you. If you have an open and honest relationship with your referees, they can even be a valuable resource when it comes to interview preparation, giving you another perspective on your strengths, professional contributions, and perhaps even your weaker areas.

Current employers are obviously a more delicate matter. If your boss knows you're job hunting and everything is out in the open then there's no issue, but often job seekers want to keep the fact they're looking for a new position under wraps until they have a firm offer on the table. It's perfectly acceptable to ask an interviewer to respect this reality. When they ask the question above, simply say something like:

I'd love you to speak to my current supervisor if I am offered the position. You let candidates know before speaking to any of their referees, I assume?

To further ensure that you're in control of the timing of any reference checks, do not provide your references' contact details along with your CV, but only separately when requested. That way, handing them over provides another opportunity to clarify timing.

93. What would you guess is the most searched-for phrase on YouTube?

The Real Question: How do you handle uncertainty? And can I get you to say something ill judged?

Top-line Tactic: *If the question halfway suggests a taboo topic, it's possible that the answer that springs to mind is the very worst answer you can give.*

Curveball questions are never about the surface wording. It follows that this particular curveball question is not about YouTube.

Believe it or not, this question does a similar job to *Tell me about yourself*. Both questions take the lid off the bubbling cauldron that is your mind. Once asked, the interviewer sits back and observes whatever floats to the surface.

But unlike *Tell me about yourself*, this question comes with an added layer of sneakiness by being mildly suggestive of naughty, not-safe-for-work themes. Everyone knows what some people are looking for on YouTube, namely the sort of thing people regularly get fired for looking at in work time.

This question tests whether you're the excitable (read: legally actionable) sort of person who will bring up taboo topics when they don't have to. Here, the taboo content is a flag being run up a flagpole; the interviewer is waiting to see if you salute it.

It doesn't matter whether you think the most searched-for phrase on YouTube is 'puppies playing in the snow' or 'One Direction' or even a pornographic term. All you need to do is mention something innocuous and then follow it up by saying that you're not exactly sure but you are confident you could find out.

Naturally you're unlikely to be asked this exact question, but you could be asked a question that works in the same way, such as *Tell me a joke*. There are interviewers who wouldn't ask for a joke in a million years, but there are some who ask for one every time. Some will ask to see if your sense of humour is similar to theirs; others will want to see if you turn potty-mouthed at the first excuse. Sadly, and as any reader of *Viz* will tell you, rude jokes are always the easiest to remember. The potential for disaster is clear, so you might want to memorize a short and entirely clean joke. Here's a handful that won't upset anyone:

Q: Why did the crab go to jail?
A: He kept pinching things.

Q: Why did the lobster blush?
A: He saw the salad dressing.

Q: What's the fastest cake in the world?
A: Scone.

A skeleton goes into a pub and asks for a pint . . . and a mop!

A penguin goes into a pub and asks the barman if he's seen his brother.
Barman: What's he look like?

They might not laugh, but laughter is not necessarily what they want from you here.

One of my colleagues at Reed even came across one interviewer who asks, *What does BMW stand for?* Google that question and you'll see that BMW can be an abbreviation for a lot of things, from an indefensible racial/sexual epithet to a comment on the reliability of BMW cars (**B**y **M**ostly **W**alking). A crafty interviewer certainly has a lot of tools to make you let your guard down. Of course, recruitment consultants would rather these questions were not an occasional fact of life, and you would probably rather not work for someone who asks one. That doesn't mean such questions aren't out there.

And as if to prove the point about avoiding taboo answers,

would you like to know what the most searched-for phrase on YouTube really is? It's *'How to . . .'*

See? I bet that wasn't what you were thinking at all . . .

94. What books and newspapers do you read?

The Real Question: Do you like to learn?

Top-line Tactic: *Tailor your answer but do not lie.*

Unless you're applying for a job in the media industry, where your taste in reading material is central to your ability to do the job well (in which case, you really shouldn't have a problem talking with knowledge and enthusiasm about your reading), this is a gentle full toss of a question. In the interviewer's mind, your reading habits are either standing in for your intelligence and curiosity or for your interest in keeping up to date in your field. They may also be probing to see if you have similar interests to the rest of the team in much the same way that teenagers use their favourite music as shorthand for their outlook. They may just be trying to relax you with small talk.

Therefore, answering this well doesn't require a well-honed strategy. Just survey the shelves of your mental library for something that this particular person is likely to connect with and answer naturally. Talking about your morning ritual of coffee and the *Financial Times* is probably going to go over better with a buttoned-up male banker than confessing your love for *Fifty Shades of Grey*.

Besides obvious howlers like the above, there are only two ways to go really wrong. The first is to lie. Who knows what your interviewer reads? If you say the latest hot novel and are then asked what you thought of the central plot twist, you're going to ruin all the good work you put into the rest of the interview. The second is to say nothing. If you can't even dredge up a single newspaper or magazine you pick up regularly, you're going to come across as uninterested in self-improvement, or to put it less politely, downright dumb.

95. Aren't you overqualified for this job?

The Real Question: Are you going to get bored and jump ship in a few months, when something better comes along?

Top-line Tactic: Reassure them that you truly want this job and will stick around.

From the candidate's perspective this can be one of the most annoying interview questions out there. Older interviewees often suspect it's ageism in disguise, while just about everyone who ends up getting asked this is irked that an employer wouldn't be thrilled to get someone with their experience.

But take a look at the situation from the employer's perspective. Hiring is time consuming and expensive, and if you hire someone for a role they can do with one hand tied behind their back, you're not crazy to worry that he or she is going to get bored and jump ship as soon as soon as something better comes along. Then you're minus the expense and energy it took to hire the person and back to square one. No wonder interviewers are desperate to avoid this outcome.

In order to reassure them, you need to tell a convincing story about why you really do want this job – offer them a motivation they can believe in and persuade them that, if hired, you'll be committed to the company. Obviously, that means avoiding any answer that smacks of desperation or boils down to simply 'I need a job!' Instead think carefully about what makes this specific position appealing to you. There's no denying the fact you're overqualified – it's written right there on your CV – the important thing is to put the situation in context. You might cite:

- **The commute:** *My current job involves two and a half miserable hours in traffic each day. I love my house and my kids are right near their school, so at this stage of my life finding a position I'm interested in and qualified for nearer to home is more important to me than title or salary.*
- **A change to career trajectory:** *I am certainly well qualified, but as you can see from my CV most of my roles have been in traditional offline marketing. I'd like to hone my online skills and I realize I may have to take a step back in order to learn a new area. Your firm seemed like a great place to put my years of experience to work and gain a new set of skills.*
- **Your passion for a particular product or project:** *Taking on slightly less responsibility is absolutely a worthwhile trade-off for me if I get to work on your ports project. I've been following the project closely and it seems like the ideal opportunity for me to put my sustainability skills to use in an exciting new context with huge growth potential.*
- **A desire for a different role:** *As I've moved into management I've found more and more of my day is taken up with meetings and reports. That's valuable work but I found I really missed the more hands-on, day-to-day tasks. That's what I'm looking to get back to.*

A heartfelt answer along these lines should go some way towards reassuring a doubtful interviewer, but there are a few more techniques that can reinforce your case. First, if your CV supports it, leverage your tenure at previous employers. If you've stayed with every past job for many years, that should count as good evidence of your loyalty and dedication.

Also, you'll want to avoid talk of salary too early. If you're overqualified the interviewer is no doubt also worried that they can't afford you. There's no benefit in scaring them off by highlighting the compensation issue before you've had a chance to sell them on your skills and motivation. After they love you, you can see if you can find common ground on the compensation issue.

96. Sell me this pen

The Real Question: Do you understand that selling is fundamentally about the customer's needs, not the product's features?

Top-line Tactic: *Go with it, have fun and make sure you address the need for the pen (or stapler, mobile phone or whatever else you're handed) more than its features.*

Have you seen the Oscar-nominated film *The Wolf of Wall Street*? In it, Leonardo DiCaprio plays a criminally greedy Wall Street titan named Jordan Belfort who accumulates (and then loses) a fortune unloading penny stocks on unsuspecting average Joes. He's a sales ace with a quirky way of evaluating fresh talent: he hands them a pen and asks them to sell it back to him.

So what's the right answer to *Sell me this pen*? In the film, a succession of mediocre sales people try to highlight the pen's outstanding features – 'This is the best pen ever made!' 'Look how smoothly it writes' and similar – but DiCaprio's Belfort is clearly unimpressed until a member of his sales team grabs the pen and hands Belfort a piece of paper.

'Write your name on the paper,' he tells Belfort, who looks around for something to write with. Now he *needs* a pen. Selling one suddenly becomes easy.

And here we come to the underlying lesson of the *Sell me a pen* exercise. Yes, it's a demonstration of showmanship and keeping a cool head under pressure, as well as a method of evaluating your approach to sales. But mostly it's a pop quiz on a fundamental principle of selling – it's about the customer's needs, not the features of the product (except, of course, in the unlikely case you're handed a truly glorious pen of actual and obvious distinction. If it's diamond encrusted, don't ignore that.)

If it's just your average disposable ballpoint, demonstrate your customer focus in your answer by highlighting the problems the object you're handed can solve. It might not be a pen but some other random thing hanging around on the interviewer's desk. Example:

Interviewee: I'm about to pull out my phone and tell you the name of a contact of mine who is in desperate need of your product.
Interviewer: I need a pen!

97. Give your CV a mark out of ten

The Real Question: Are you thoughtful and strategic about your job search (because then you have a good chance of being thoughtful and strategic about your job)?

Top-line Tactic: *The rating matters less than how you explain it.*

The dangers of this question are immediately apparent. Instantly give your CV a ten and you sound cocky and disinclined to improve. Give it a five and you've just told the interviewer you are a mediocre candidate when he or she is almost certainly hoping for a standout. So how do you wriggle out of the difficulty?

As with other curveball questions, the point of interest here is not so much your answer as evaluating your ability to think on your feet when confronted with a truly tough question. For that reason, your approach here should be similar to other puzzle-type questions: choose a number (yes, a pretty high one is probably a good idea) and explain step-by-step how you arrived at that conclusion.

Let me think about that for a minute . . . Well, I suppose it depends how you look at it. In the sense that a CV is designed to get you the interview and I'm sitting here now, I'd have to give it a ten. But there are other criteria you could use to judge a CV. I don't feel like I've peaked in my career yet, for instance, so I expect my CV to become stronger as I develop new skills and strengthen old ones. In that sense, there's room for improvement, so I'd give it maybe a seven. At the moment, I feel I'm an exceptional mid-level manager but I have the potential to do much more. Overall, I'd give it an eight or a nine.

This question is closely related to another favourite: rate your *career* out of ten. Related, but not quite the same. When asked to rate your CV, it's OK to give the slightly cheeky ten out of ten mentioned above, because your CV really is just a piece of paper designed to get you in the door. By contrast, your career is a much more weighty subject; a flippant approach to rating it won't help you.

That's not to say you still shouldn't give your career a high mark, more that you need to draw their attention to what it is you're rating. You'll make a much better impression if you rate your career in terms of *your contribution to your employers or your customers*, be that in widgets sold or babies midwifed or whatever your expected output is supposed to be. Talking about what you did to help somebody will go over much better than exulting in markers of progress that only mean something to individuals, such as promotions and pay rises. More experienced candidates could top off this question by pointing to any examples of them giving back to the industry, be it great or small – seminars, publications, training roles, internships, speeches, thought leadership etc. Giving back is always rewarding; if your career includes it then it deserves a high mark indeed.

98. Our product has seriously antisocial side effects. How do you feel about that?

The Real Question: Are you a responsible person? Can you weigh up the benefits and risks of the product and set them into context?

Top-line Tactic: *Don't assume they don't care about social impact.*

Every society keeps a list of industries that, morally speaking, have some explaining to do. It's a list that goes beyond the usual suspects like armaments, tobacco and alcohol.

These days, firms can attract criticism for products as diverse as sugary drinks, fast cars, tuna, gambling, pharmaceuticals, fossil fuels, luxury property, or anything advertised to children. Almost every firm must now think about its social footprint and the debate surrounding such issues can turn on a sixpence.

You might think that firms prefer to hire people who have no problem with what the firm sells, and on one level you'd be right – but more often employers want to know that they're hiring a well-rounded person who can see both sides.

The Q&A website Quora carries an account from an individual who interviewed for a job in weapons procurement for the US Navy. He was asked how he felt about the fact that those weapons would be used to kill people. He answered that he didn't feel good about that *at all* – and got the job. The navy thought of him as one of the normal ones. It seems the armed forces don't want gun nuts; it's not hard to see why. The more bullets they fire, the more intense bombardment they attract.

It follows that when you're asked about an employer's controversial activities, please understand that they're not just looking for hard-headed realists. It pays to have a heart. Acknowledge that every product has downsides that must be addressed. For example, don't assume that no one in the drinks industry cares about alcoholism – it's quite likely they'll want to know what you think about anti-alcoholism initiatives such as the Portman Group.

99. How many traffic lights are there in London?

The Real Question: How do you think through tough problems?

Top-line Tactic: *Puzzle it out step by step . . . out loud.*

This specific sort of curveball question is known as a brainteaser, and if you are asked one in an interview you can blame Google. The search giant and other top Silicon Valley firms popularized the idea of asking candidates to solve wacky riddles. The traffic lights in London question is only one example of many such questions. Others include:

- If you were hired to wash all the windows in Leeds, how much would you charge?
- How many 10 pence pieces – placed one on top of the other – would it take to reach the top of the Shard?
- How many piano tuners are there in Glasgow?
- Why are manhole covers round?
- How would you move Mount Fuji? (Yes, really.)

The irony is that Google actually stopped asking these sorts of questions, as they found that they have no ability to predict job performance, but when your interviewer asks you to count piano tuners or traffic lights probably isn't the best time to point this out.

So how should you proceed? First, reassure yourself that no one has all the necessary information at his or her disposal to accurately answer any of these questions. The interviewer who asks how many golf balls will fit inside a jumbo jet isn't expecting you to be both an aerospace engineer and a measurement-obsessed golf fanatic. What they are expecting of you is the ability to logically attack the question, picking it apart into the information you need and doing your best to either estimate the answer or tell them where you could locate it.

Because the process is the important part here, take a breath to gather your thoughts and then simply walk the interviewer through your thinking out loud, making sure to ask for any necessary clarifications. For the Shard question, for example, you might inquire whether your coins are to be stacked face to face or edge to edge.

The answer to the London traffic light question might go something like this:

Hmmm . . . I couldn't give you an exact number, obviously, but I could make a guess by trying to estimate the number of traffic lights in a square mile based on my personal experience and then taking a shot at the total size of London in square miles.

Of course, there would be more traffic lights in the centre than in the suburbs, but I reckon that would average out. It would probably be quicker just to Google it, though.

The point is to show you're considering the constituent parts of the question and able to come up with creative ways to solve them. If you have no idea of the total area of London, maybe you could guesstimate how long it would take you to trek from one end to the other and divide by your average walking speed. Is that likely to be accurate? Of course not. But that's not the point.

(A cautionary note: If you're interviewing at a software firm, research institute or investment bank where maths skills are highly prized, accuracy and sophistication is going to count a lot more than if you're hoping to win a job that's far less quantitative, so don't take the idea that 'the answer doesn't matter' too far in such cases.)

100. What haven't I asked you that I should have?

The Real Question: Person to person, who are you behind the mask?

Top-line tactic: *You've intrigued – or possibly baffled – the interviewer. Just be genuine.*

Is this the world's laziest interview question? Maybe, but if your interviewer is asking you to come up with the questions, there may be another explanation besides lack of preparation.

If the interviewer is pulling this less than common trick out of the bag midway through the interview, it may be because you're giving the impression that there is more to you than has so far been uncovered. Your answers may be polished and well prepared, for example, but the people sitting on the other side of the table feel they're not really glimpsing the real you. Like 'curveballs', the point of asking you to come up with the questions may simply be to destabilize you sufficiently for your mask to slip and reveal a little bit of the human underneath.

On the other hand, the motivation for asking this question may be simple respect. You, after all, know far more about your skills, aspirations, experience and passions than the interviewer. If the person asking the questions has reached a point where they trust you and are generally intrigued by your answers, they may pass you the baton and offer you the chance to leverage that information asymmetrically. The interviewer, in other words, may genuinely believe that you know better what you should be talking about and trust you to steer the conversation in a productive and revealing direction. That's a great sign!

Finally, if this question comes at the very end of the interview it may be exactly what it seems – an invitation to add anything you're burning to tell the interviewer but haven't yet had a chance to discuss.

So how should you respond? That's simple. Ride out any initial shock by taking as much time as you need to consider the question (this may feel like an awkwardly long pause but that's OK) and then just answer genuinely. Do you have a great skill or quality you want to highlight? Then say: *You should ask me about the Ruby on Rails workshop I took last summer*, or, *You should ask me about how quickly I can turn around design projects*. Is there a project that you're super-proud of that you haven't yet highlighted? Then go ahead and suggest you talk about that.

Maybe you're more keen to discuss some aspect of the role or company. Try saying: *We should talk about my ideas for the Japan initiative*, or *I'd love to chat about how to counter the threat from competitor X*. The point here is to be honest – suggest a topic you are genuinely interested in and one, obviously, that will paint you in a positive light considering the qualities and skills needed for the role.

101. When can you start?

The Real Question: Is your current employer going to make a counter-offer? Are you going to resign without a thought for the hassle it will cause – either there or, one day, here?

Top-line Tactic: *Quote your contractual notice period. Go easy on the sabbaticals.*

'When can you start?' sounds a lot like 'We're going to offer you the job', but of course it's not the same thing, so if you hear it in interview be careful you don't suddenly start acting like you own the place. Indeed, some interviewers, when faced with a likeable but hopeless candidate, will ask this question merely to make small talk and pad out the allotted time, so it is by no means always good news.

But assuming they like you and genuinely want to know the answer, and assuming that you're already in a job, there really is only one polite thing you can say: you'll be starting as soon as your current notice period ends. You might be tempted to ask for time off between jobs, but that is tantamount to saying that you know they're going to make you an offer; it's also a way of saying that your energy levels are perhaps not all they could be.

Most importantly, the interviewer will want to see some evidence (a) that you're going to extricate yourself from your current employer with the maximum decency and consideration and (b) that you really do plan to quit, since some candidates pretend they're on the job market when they're simply looking to squeeze a better offer out of their current employer.

For both eventualities, the only reassuring answer you can give is that you'd have to work your full notice period if required, but that you'd be looking forward to joining the hirer at the earliest opportunity.

SEVEN

PARTING SHOTS

When it's your turn

Answering interview questions is stressful, but at least you have the advantage of knowing what you're trying to accomplish – you're trying to present your skills and personal qualities in the best possible light. But what about that moment which comes at the end of almost every interview, when the interviewer turns the tables and invites you to ask questions of your own?

Rather than feeling they're in the driver's seat, this moment is seen as an invitation to panic by many interviewees. You might wonder: *What exactly is expected of me here? What am I trying to get out of this phase of the interview?*

If that's you, forgive yourself: your confusion is justified. What makes this situation so fraught is the tension between what everyone in the room is *pretending* is going on and what is *really* going on.

Despite surface appearances, this phase of the interview isn't primarily about gathering additional information about the company or your role, though of course any additional facts or impressions will certainly be useful if they make an offer. Instead, this is a time for you to tie up the interview with a bow and exhibit some personal charm, a time to demonstrate you're knowledgeable about the company and have been paying close attention to the conversation. That will close your case for being the best candidate for the job, and leave the interviewer with a favourable impression.

You're supposedly just soliciting information, but really you're trying to simultaneously show off and be charming – and both you and interviewer know it but can't say it. No wonder this bit stresses everyone out!

Adding to the tension is a psychological bias known as the peak-end rule. Memorably illustrated by Nobel prize-winning psychologist Daniel Kahneman in his book *Thinking, Fast and Slow*, this bias means that when we remember a past event our impression of it is disproportionately influenced by the final moments of the experience.

Whether the event is massively unpleasant – such as a painful colonoscopy in one experiment cited by Kahneman – or totally enjoyable – such as the spring holidays another study looked at – our recollections are strongly coloured by our final impressions. End on a painful note and the entire procedure is recalled as painful, even if the majority of the time it was only mildly uncomfortable. Have a great last day on your beach holiday and you'll recall the whole trip fondly, even if you spent the previous six days of the week bickering with your partner or regretting your failure to apply sunscreen.

What's true for medical tests and vacations is true for interviews too. The question-and-answer phase is a unique opportunity to leave a strong and long-lasting impression on your interviewer.

So what are you trying to accomplish?

We've established that the endgame isn't as simple as it first appears and can't be neglected. The next question is how we might dial back the pressure so you can perform at your peak.

To do so requires three things:

- understanding your objectives
- preparation
- reading your interviewer

Let's take those one by one. Whatever role you're applying for, some aspects of the question section remain the same. This is, as already mentioned, decidedly not just about gathering additional information. You are being tested here on your familiarity with the company, your poise and self-salesmanship. You'll improve your chances of performing well by keeping those principles firmly in mind.

With that understanding as your foundation, the next essential ingredient is to prepare ahead of time. There are plenty of suggested questions to come later in the chapter to help you out. After perusing them and pondering both what you may actually want to know about the role and company and which points about your skills or background you especially want to stress, jot down five or six short, straightforward questions a day or two before your interview. (No one appreciates a rambler and simple questions are easier to remember.)

You probably won't get to ask all of those questions, but it's important *to start with more than you'll need* for a couple of reasons. First, you'll probably eliminate some of them well ahead of the interview. Take your list of questions and see if you can find the answer to any of them with a few minutes of Googling. If you can, cross that question off the list.

Remember, one of your goals for the question-and-answer section is to demonstrate your research and knowledge of the company. If the answer to your question is plastered across the top of the firm's homepage, you may as well have come into the interview wearing a sandwich board saying, 'I didn't bother to prepare.' In addition, by poking around on the company's website and reading recent news articles about the organization, you might find fodder for more thoughtful questions about recent initiatives, changes or significant challenges the company is facing.

Commit your Google-vetted list of questions to memory. It's not necessary to remember them word for word, but the adrenalin may be pumping on the day, so you want to make sure at least a few possibilities are lodged firmly in your brain. If you're really worried about blanking under pressure, jot a couple of memory-jogging doodles on the folder in which you'll bring your CV and references to the interview.

Whatever strategies you employ to memorize things, keep in mind there is little worse than a candidate who responds to *Do you have any questions for me?* with a quick *Nope, I've got all the information I need, thanks*. Fail to ask any questions and you convey to the interviewer some unfortunate combination of lack of curiosity, disinterest in the job or company and/or general absence of social graces.

Which questions should I ask?

So far the advice on asking questions has applied no matter what industry, role or type of interviewer you're facing, but there can be no hard and fast rules about what specific questions to ask that span all possible situations. (Though there are some things you should NEVER ask, listed later in the chapter.) The questions you end up asking obviously depend in part on what is covered in the interview. If possible, explicitly link your questions to topics that came up earlier, as in:

You mentioned that you hold an annual sales conference. Is there scope in this role to eventually get involved in the planning of that event?

Or perhaps:

Earlier you characterized the management style here as 'collaborative'. What sort of candidates do you find thrive in this sort of environment?

These questions indicate you've been paying careful attention. Everyone appreciates being listened to.

If there's an area in which you feel you excel, and you think the interviewer doesn't yet have the full picture of your abilities, your choice of question could also be used to direct the conversation to those areas where you're strong. For instance, you could ask whether a certain characteristic or skill is important for this role. If the interviewer responds positively, you've just created an opening to explain your qualifications and experience in that area in more detail.

Another consideration is the personal style of the interviewer. Some are uncomfortable and stiff, others relaxed and informal. Asking a buttoned-up type gentle personal questions about their own experience at the company may put them at ease and establish a stronger personal connection. Interviewers are, of course, as diverse as any other group of human beings. Some appreciate being challenged, others prefer buddy-buddy camaraderie. Some are formal, others more relaxed. Some appreciate a direct question about their impressions of your application while others may react to that with discomfort. No book can provide a magic formula to navigate all these differences, but if you keep in mind your objectives – conveying your skills, demonstrating interest and creating a personal connection – all while remaining open to the social style of your interviewer, you have the best possible chance of using the question phase of the interview to your advantage.

Question inspiration

The types of questions you might ask fall into five broad categories. These are questions about the role, the team, the company, the interviewer and your own performance (this last is a bit of a special category and not for the faint of heart). There are also some questions you should always ask, and others you should steer well clear of. We'll go through the categories one by one before offering examples to help you brainstorm questions of your own that fit your specific situation.

Questions about the role

If you get the gig, you'll actually have to do the job, so it's natural to show a healthy interest in the challenges, objectives and day-to-day realities of the role. Asking questions like these shows you are genuinely keen on the position and serious about succeeding within it.

> *How does this position fit into the overall management structure?*
> *What skills or qualities do you feel are needed to succeed in this role? or What sort of person has succeeded in this role in the past?*
> *What is the main problem this role needs to solve?*
> *Should I get the job, what are the top priorities I'd be focusing on?*

What are the biggest challenges of this role?

What sort of training, professional development or support will be available to me?

Is there scope for career development with this role?

(Note: when asking questions along these lines make sure you're coming across as eager to learn and contribute, rather than overly ambitious and keen to leave the position for greener pastures at the earliest opportunity.)

What would success look like? In this job, how will success be judged?

What results would you expect me to achieve in the first six months? or What is the timeline for success in this role?

Why has the position become available?

(If it's a new role:) *Why was the position created?*

(If someone left the role:) *Why did they leave or what did they go on to do?*

What is the typical career trajectory for this position?

What does a typical day look like?

Can you show me any examples of projects I'd be working on?

Do you expect the responsibilities of this role to evolve?

Consider the last few individuals to have done this job. What separates the best from the worst?

Questions about the team

A dream job can quickly turn into a nightmare if you dislike those you're working with or if you don't fit in with the company culture.

The following questions help you assess how you'll fit in with your immediate co-workers and present yourself as a team player who is an ideal fit for the existing culture.

What are the top two personality traits someone would need to fit in here?

How large is the team I will be working with?

Can you tell me about the team I will be working with?

Who will I be reporting to directly?

How would you characterize the communication style of the team I'll be working with? or *How would you characterize the work style of the team I'll be working with?*

Will I have the opportunity to meet my manager/those I will be managing? (Depending on the position)

Do you hold team-building events?

Is the team personally close knit? Do members of the team socialize outside the office?

Which primary clients will I be working with? (If appropriate; some industries or companies put a premium on confidentiality and discretion) or *What kind of clients will I be working with?*

What other teams work most closely with this one?

Questions about the company

These sorts of questions are ideal for demonstrating your knowledge about the industry, as well as recent developments at the organization. This is the place to put that Googling to good use.

Are there any plans for expansion?

Do you expect X company or industry trend to continue into the next quarter/year?

You recently introduced X product/service/division. How will this affect the organization?

What are the most important goals the company is focused on currently?

How would you describe the company culture?

What is the turnover of staff like throughout the company?

What's the most important feature that distinguishes this company from its competitors?

This company/industry is facing X challenge. How are you responding?

Tell me something about the company that it would otherwise take six months to learn.

Questions about the interviewer

Not everyone who interviews likes interviewing (nor, frankly, is everyone good at it). If you sense your interviewer is uncomfortable, asking them for their personal take on professional matters (not, of course, just for their recommendation for a place to eat lunch) may help to loosen them up and create a closer personal bond.

What's the best thing about working at your company?
What's different about working here from companies you've worked with in the past?
How has the company changed since you joined?
Why do you like working here?
Where do you see the company heading? or *How do you see the company evolving over the next five years?*

Questions about your performance

These sorts of questions aren't for everyone – and that goes both for candidates and interviewers. Directly asking about your performance in the interview can work, but only if you have the sort of personality that can carry such a question off and the confidence to respond cogently to criticism. This approach can also backfire if you have an interviewer with a less direct, more laid-back style who may be put off by your hard sell. So use these with caution.

Do you have any concerns about my qualifications that I could address?
Do you have any worries about my suitability for the role?
How do I compare to your ideal candidate?

*Is there anything you have seen in the other people on the shortlist
that you have not seen in me?*

Questions about next steps

If the last section involved questions you should think hard
about before asking, this section offers the types of questions
you should absolutely always ask, every time, in every interview. The only exception would perhaps be if you have a
recruiter following up on your behalf, but even then it never
hurts to nail down the next steps.

What are the next steps in the interview process?
Can I provide you with anything else that would be helpful?
What happens next?
When do you think you'll be making a decision?

Questions you should never ask

The objective of the foregoing questions is to telegraph your
excitement about the role. Conversely, asking about logistical
details makes it seem like your interest is contingent on pension schemes and flexible work policies. Maybe it is. But this
isn't the place to let that show. *Save those sorts of questions for
further along in the hiring process.*

Also, steer clear of any sort of question that could paint
you in a bad light, i.e. as mercenary, a gossip or plain clueless.
For example:

What's the salary?
What is it exactly that you do?
I heard X piece of gossip about this company/employee. Is it true?
How much time off will I get?
Is there a pension scheme?

Can I work part-time? or *Is there the opportunity for a flexible schedule/telecommuting/a job share?*

How soon can I get promoted?

Can I use Facebook at work?

Money, money, money

The first thing to say about money is that if the salary range is stated in the job ad, and is not enough for you, then don't apply. You should not plan to get an offer and then start negotiating. As the hiring firm sees it, those negotiations were concluded when you applied for the job. You'd be livid if they dropped the salary offer after putting it into the ad, so why do the same thing to them in reverse?

If the salary is negotiable, but you absolutely, positively *hate* the idea of bargaining, you can always ask if your recruitment consultant is prepared do it for you. Some will, some won't, but it never hurts to ask. Certainly it's something many will have done before, and so they tend to have a good idea of the going rate.

But if you'd rather negotiate your own way, and there are no clues in the ad, what follows in this next section will seem like either useful advice or a teeth-grinding chore. That's because a person's relationship to money goes deep down, like politics or sex or religion, and many of us are wary of discussing those things with a complete stranger. Certainly, many of us would rather not have to negotiate money if we can avoid it.

And avoiding it is no sin. Money needn't be everything, and to many people it isn't. They're happy just to be on their way to pastures new, certainly happy enough to take the job at the stated salary. They don't want to risk having the job offer withdrawn simply because they were asking for too much money, something which can and does happen – especially if the hirer misinterprets your negotiations as a sign that you're motivated mainly by money. Data from Salary. com shows that 87 per cent of companies won't pull a job offer if a candidate negotiates. But that means 13 per cent will. How terrifying to you is the prospect of being in that 13 per cent? You need to take your own temperature on that.

Naturally, if you always pass on the chance to negotiate money, over the course of a career you could be passing up a significant sum. It's impossible to say how much, as everybody's situation is different, but the principle is clear.

Many people simply don't know how to negotiate their salary or hate the process. But with a little guidance, negotiating need not be so intimidating or so unpleasant.

Preparation is everything

As with so much else in this book, when it comes to negotiating your salary and benefits, preparation is key. While exactly how and when to introduce the topic of salary is slightly controversial, you can be assured that the topic will come up. The company you are interviewing with views you as an asset that they would potentially like to acquire. As with any other asset, they will be keen to get the best possible price, and in this case that means the lowest compensation package you will accept.

Knowing that, it's your responsibility to establish the going rate for the job. Getting this sort of information used to be tricky, but thanks to the internet it's now quite straightforward. Free sites like PayScale, Salary and Glassdoor can provide decent data on the talent market in your area.

Of course, getting a handle on the going rates for talent won't benefit you if you don't have a realistic sense of your own skill level and the seniority of the job you're applying for. In many areas of life, bluster pays – but when it comes to salary negotiations, its value is limited. Confidence never hurt anyone, but you stand a much better chance of coming to a mutually satisfactory arrangement with your new employer if you have an accurate sense of your experience, skills and the demands of the role.

After you've armed yourself with the latest data on the market and taken a long, hard look at your own qualifications, the final step in your pre-interview preparation is to set three numbers firmly in your mind. First, what's your ideal salary? If all goes swimmingly, what number are you hoping to hear? Next is your no-go number. At what point will you simply walk away from the offer as it fails to meet your needs? The range between these two figures is the third number to keep in mind – call it the satisfactory range.

The other kind of prep

You have your ideal, no-go and satisfactory range all set, so you have everything you need to combat whatever the interviewer throws at you, right? Unfortunately, no. While nuts-and-bolts information on the talent market and an honest assessment of your place in it are essential preparation, they're not sufficient.

In addition to taking a look at the market and yourself, you also need to think carefully about the role and the company where you are applying. Workplaces will differ in their flexibility when it comes to negotiating compensation. If you're applying for a public sector or unionized job, there may be very strict rules about pay that leave the person hiring you with very little room to manoeuvre. In this respect, joining a small charity or the public sector is very different from a sales role at a hectic medium-sized company. Your approach to negotiating needs to take account of this. Advocate on your own behalf, but be realistic about the internal constraints faced by the other side.

If you are applying for a very senior position, you may also face another internal constraint known as internal equity. It's difficult (or maybe even impossible) to hire someone at a vastly higher salary than to others at a similar level, or at a salary close to those above them in the hierarchy. If you're at this level, keep in mind that these issues may be foremost in the mind of the person hiring you.

Putting it into practice

No matter how well equipped with information you are, the salary negotiation tussle still requires a light touch.

Traditionally, job seekers have generally been advised to make sure they are never the first to bring up the topic of salary. There are a couple of reasons for this. First, if you start talking about money and benefits too early, you risk coming across as mercenary. With the possible exception of commission-based sales roles, hunger for money is generally not an attractive quality in a job candidate. If an extra pound is all you care about, what's stopping you from leaving this company when another marginally more lucrative offer comes along? Second, when interviewers try to get you to talk about your salary requirements or salary history relatively early in the interview process, they're generally trying to screen you out either as too expensive or too junior-level. Complying with that has little upside for you.

Also, if you name a number first, you run the risk of throwing out a figure significantly lower than the company would have been willing to pay. Thanks to the anchoring effect – a principle by which the first number mentioned sets the expected range for discussion in a negotiation – you can create a situation where getting to a fair compensation package is an uphill battle.

Best, then, to try and let the interviewer raise the subject, and ideally to put the conversation off entirely until after an offer is on the table that you haven't yet accepted. This is when you'll have the most leverage, because the company is clearly interested in you. But, be warned, interviewers most assuredly know this advice is out there, and many of them will try to push you into throwing out a number well before that point.

If possible, deflect them. There are several approaches that might work. You can try deflecting the question with a question. If the interviewer asks, for instance, *What are your salary expectations?* you can respond with something like, *Yes, we haven't discussed compensation yet. I'm interested to learn more about that. Can you fill me in on whether you have a particular range in mind?* Alternately, you might try and leave the matter open by stating you don't yet feel you have enough information about the role and responsibilities to answer, or claim that you'd like to do a bit more research now that you have a better understanding of what the job entails.

When the question is phrased as an inquiry into your current salary, you can deflect the issue by letting the interviewer know you feel your current role and the role you are interviewing for are perhaps different, and therefore you don't feel your salary information is particularly relevant. If there is no escaping their inquiries about your salary history, consider revealing what you earn but with the same caveat.

Similarly, when a persistent interviewer corners you into revealing your salary expectations, phrase your answer as a range, i.e. *I am focusing my search on jobs in the X–Y range*, or *I'm being interviewed for jobs paying in the range of X–Y.* This is the time to use the ideal number you prepared earlier. If you're hesitant, remember the anchoring effect. Lowballing yourself here will only make the task of negotiating fair compensation down the road harder.

If all these deflection techniques pay off, or your interviewer has simply not pushed the matter of compensation early in the process, how should you broach the subject later on? There are two schools of thought on that.

If you are moving along in the interview process and are convinced the company is very keen on hiring you, you could get out in front of the situation and raise the subject yourself. Perhaps you have been called back for another round of interviews. At this stage, you might ask the recruiter or HR executive you are dealing with if now is a good time to talk about your compensation. When he or she asks you about your past compensation, inform her of the range you are looking for. It may sound aggressive, but for advocates of the practice this approach has the advantage of anchoring the discussion at a number of your choosing and gives you more leverage should the offer come back lower than your stated expectations.

For many junior job candidates this approach may be far too aggressive. Instead, more conservative candidates can follow traditional advice and wait for the company to make a firm offer that includes compensation. At this stage, even if you're more risk averse, unless the offer blows your socks off, consider negotiating. Most employers expect you to and won't be put off. Of course, any attempt to move the number should be done in a pleasant and flexible fashion.

What if your requests are repeatedly met with insistence that the salary can't be changed? This is the time to be flexible and look at the whole package, including benefits, to see if you can move towards agreement. If the budget genuinely can't accommodate the salary you want, could you get an additional week's holiday? How about an accelerated review at six months where your performance could earn you a quicker increase? Or maybe a signing-on bonus could get you closer to your ideal salary with your performance speaking for itself next year? Would the company be open to a day of telecommuting a week? Perhaps even a four-day week? There's no suggestion that you should ask for any of these things in particular, but they show that there is more than one way to compensate you. Stay flexible and pleasant and you're most likely to end up with an offer that meets everyone's needs.

Last impressions – how to wrap up the interview

First impressions may be incredibly important and hard to erase, but as Kahneman showed us earlier, last impressions count too. Aside from that first, intuitive sense of a job seeker, the next most likely thing an interviewer will recall about a candidate is his or her most recent interaction with the individual, i.e. the final moments of the interview process. That means you can't relax just because your forty-five minutes are up and you've just asked the hiring manager the last of your carefully prepared questions.

How you finish the interview and follow up afterwards can make or break your candidacy, but don't worry. This section will outline the pitfalls of wrapping up an interview and guide you to ensure your last interactions with a company are as impressive as all your previous efforts to wow them, starting from the moment the question-and-answer phase of the discussion finishes and moving along until you learn the fate of your application.

To close or not to close?

While there are essential points of interview etiquette nearly everyone agrees on, there are also huge disagreements among experts about the right approach to ending an interview. Chief among them is 'the close'. It's standard sales practice to ask explicitly for the sale at the end of a conversation, though techniques range from subtle nudges to high-pressure insistence. Should you 'close' your interview as well?

There's absolutely no harm and plenty of benefit to be gained from explicitly telling your interviewer that you're very interested in the position and think you'd be a great fit for it, offering two or three brief points as to why. Pretty much every candidate should say something along these lines before they leave the interview room. Something succinct and straightforward is generally a good option:

Thanks so much for taking the time to interview me today. Based on our discussion, this sounds like just the sort of position I was looking for. I believe my background and skills would be a great fit and I could really benefit your organization. I'd love to join the team, if you'll have me.

Depending on the situation, you can jazz up this basic close by complimenting the company, citing a previous project or accomplishment that you think makes you a particularly strong candidate, or even by dropping in a mention of another job you've been offered to show you're in high demand.

If you're a bolder type applying for a job that requires confidence and salesmanship, you can take things a step further by asking the interviewer if they have any reservations about your candidacy. The advantages of this approach are clear – if you know the company's concerns you can address them directly and hopefully overcome them. The dangers are equally apparent. It takes boldness to pull off and also an interviewer who is game. It's not hard to imagine a question like this making a less experienced or shyer interviewer uncomfortable. As ever, you need to pay attention to the cues coming from across the table and pitch your style to suit theirs.

Don't leave the room without . . .

As in every other area of job interviewing, there is no definitive consensus on how to conduct yourself in the final stages of the interview process. Some experts advocate a strong, 'sales-like' close and an active approach to following up. Others essentially associate this with inauthenticity or, in the extreme, badgering. We'll get to those controversies later and offer guidance on how you can feel your way towards the appropriate approach for your particular situation, but first there are a few 'must dos' every job seeker should keep in mind.

Ensure you explicitly ask your interviewer about next steps and the timeline for the hiring process. A simple, 'Can you tell me about the next steps in the interview process?' possibly followed up with 'When do you expect a decision to be made?' should arm you with valuable information about when you can expect to hear back. Also, make sure you have a business card so that you have your interviewer's complete contact information.

In this age of social media, some experts recommend asking the hiring manager to connect on LinkedIn. This is very dependent on the depth of the rapport you've developed and the personal style of the interviewer. If you've had an engaging chat with a seemingly tech-savvy interviewer who treats you like a peer, this might be a good idea, particularly if you've discussed industry trends or other topics and can plausibly claim you might want to send interesting materials or continue the discussion later online. If the interviewer was very formal or distant, think very carefully before suggesting an online connection as they may construe the request as awkward or pushy.

These logistics taken care of, all that's left is for you to make a pleasant exit. The same advice that goes for the beginning, goes for the end. Smile and give the interviewer a firm handshake. (Never, ever apologize if you think you performed less than your best.) Thank them for their time and off you go.

Don't forget a warm goodbye for the receptionist on the way out. It's only a matter of good manners, of course – but, also, in smaller workplaces that same receptionist will often rush into the interview room as soon as you've gone and ask your interviewer how it went. Don't think they won't chip in with their own thoughts.

The thank-you note conundrum

Second only to the controversy about 'closing' is the question of the thank-you note.

There's no argument about whether you should send one – a CareerBuilder survey found that 15 per cent of hiring managers would completely dismiss your candidacy if you failed to send one, while a further 32 per cent would think less of you.

A thank you of some kind is a must, but some people will advise you to send a handwritten note on the theory that you'll stand out, while others will say this comes across as desperate. These naysayers advocate a simple email instead.

Like everyone else, your interviewer is busy and will begin to be bombarded with tasks, requests and questions the second he or she walks out of the interview room – all of which will quickly begin to erode memories of you. For this reason, speed really counts and makes email generally the better bet. But again, this is a question of personal style, so take the temperature of the interviewer. Does he or she seem like the type to be impressed by an actual paper letter? If so, don't cling to the standard email advice.

Just whatever you do, don't use Facebook message or send a text message. One day, new forms of communication may overtake traditional channels in much the way email has largely overtaken the handwritten note – but that day has not yet arrived. For the time being, connecting by social media or text will make you appear inexperienced and unprofessional. It's less clear whether you might use the occasion to connect with your interviewer on LinkedIn, but you should probably wait until their decision is known before even thinking about it.

What should your thank-you note contain? Essentially the same thing as your close, so use the level of directness you chose for your verbal clincher as a guide to exactly how to phrase your thank-you note. It helps to mention a few key points of the interview: *As we discussed, the role emphasizes new customer development, which is one of my strengths*, or *I was particularly excited to learn about the new facility you will be opening. I believe my skillset is ideal for establishing a new team from the ground up . . .*

Be sure also to hit on your enthusiasm for the job and a couple of key reasons you think you'd excel in the position. Just remember: everyone is busy, keep it short.

How to follow up without being a stalker

You ended your interview strongly and quickly followed up with a brief but compelling thank-you note. Now comes the waiting . . . and the wondering about whether and when to follow up. There's no controversy here. Everyone's advice boils down to the same thing: do your best to stay top of your interviewer's mind without pestering or coming across as a stalker.

But while the principle is clear, applying it is harder.

A good rule of thumb is to follow the lead of the interviewer in terms of both timing and method of communication. Hopefully, you asked about the timeline for the next stages of the interview process at the end of your interview. If the interviewer said that they were hoping to make a decision in two weeks, it's perfectly reasonable to reach out after that deadline has passed and say:

You mentioned you were hoping to make a decision by the fifteenth, so I wanted to check the progress of my application. I am still very interested in the position, so please let me know if I can provide any additional information that would help you reach a decision.

Perhaps you will quickly hear back that there is some internal hold-up (this is very common) and they expect things to take another week or two. Consider that as encouragement. It's unlikely that they would bother to keep you informed if you weren't in the running and feel free to politely check in again should the time period they mention pass without further word. However, it's also possible that after sending a thank-you note and a quick follow-up you receive radio silence. Now is the time to muster all your willpower and resist getting back in touch.

Think about this situation as similar to dating. If you call someone and they don't call you back, you might try one more time. After that, the general consensus is you're just being annoying if you continue to call. If they wanted to get back to you they would have. Interview follow-up involves similar principles. There is nothing to be gained in pestering, badgering or borderline stalking. As with dating, this can be difficult and, as with dating, the same advice applies. Don't sit by the phone! Continue getting your CV out there, keep up your networking efforts and prepare to move on. Think carefully about whether you actually want the job. Keep busy and the waiting is easier.

As well as following the interviewer's lead when it comes to the timing of your follow-up, you should also let them guide you as to their preferred means of communication. Generally, it's best to follow past practice: if they usually email, you should too; if they seem to prefer quick telephone calls, pick up the phone. A word of caution: these days many job ads specifically ask candidates not to call. They're not being clever; this isn't a test of your initiative or gumption. They really find calls annoying. So, *don't call*.

One final word about waiting: you may hear during this time that the company has contacted your referees. Should you take this as a sign you're about to be offered the job? Unfortunately the answer is no. While it definitely does mean you're one of the top handful of candidates, many companies will check the references of several front-runners. Be encouraged, but don't draw any conclusions.

It's a no . . . or nothing

Some people are just plain rude and, sadly, that extends to hiring managers. Simply waiting and waiting and not hearing back from a company is unfortunately fairly common – some employment surveys suggest that well over half of all job seekers have experienced a deafening silence following a job interview. There's no good excuse for this sort of behaviour on the part of the company, but that doesn't make it unusual.

Being stuck in post-interview limbo can be hugely

frustrating. Try not to let it get to you. The internal process of selecting a candidate and all the attendant HR processes often take much longer than candidates expect, so a longish wait doesn't necessarily spell death for your chances, but if weeks become months and you've still had no word from the company, it's time to just let it go. Don't take the snub personally. There are dozens of reasons for companies not to hire you, from a vague gut sense that you weren't the right fit to internal concerns like budget issues or personnel reshuffles. Rejection is part of the process – even if that rejection is not overtly communicated to you – so even though it's difficult, try not to be discouraged.

This advice applies equally well to cases where the company does the right thing and calls to tell you that you weren't selected. At least in this case, if they offer you feedback on your performance or a rationale for their decision, you can use that information to improve your interviewing skills next time. But keep in mind that interviewing is a process of matching, which is designed to pair up candidates and companies that are a good fit for one another. Just because you were not the best fit with this particular company, doesn't mean there's anything necessarily wrong with you. They may simply be looking for a detail-oriented person to nail execution while you are a big-picture strategic thinker. There's nothing that needs changing about either of you – you were just not a match.

If it's a yes

Congratulations! It's never been easy to land a job, so you must have applied the principles in this book and given an impressive performance at your interview to be offered the position.

Now's the time to use the compensation negotiation tips we spoke about earlier!

The real answer

At first glance this appears to be a book about job interviews, but as you hopefully understood from the introduction, it's actually about happiness and self-fulfilment. It is in the name of self-fulfilment that you should seek to land your dream job, not because it's high status, high paying or will impress your mum.

Your dream job is your dream job because it is right for you. In other words, it will make your life happier.

Still not convinced? A research team at Harvard University took their investigation of the link between work and life satisfaction to the extreme. The Grant Study, steered for much of its course by psychiatrist George Vaillant, followed 268 men who graduated from the university in the early 1940s for their entire adult lives – an impressive seventy-five years. What did the reams and reams of data generated by this unprecedented study reveal about the link between life satisfaction and professional achievement?

Money wasn't particularly important. Neither was status or power. What did matter was a personal fit between the man and his work.

'We found that contentment in the late seventies was not even suggestively associated with parental social class or even the man's own income,' Vaillant commented. 'In terms of achievement, the only thing that matters is that you be content at your work.'

The key to professional happiness isn't winning the

international acclaim of Andy Summers or the riches of Richard Branson. It's finding the right job *for you*. Understand this fundamental truth of job hunting – that it's a process of matching your abilities and preferences to the needs of an employer – and two important truths become clear.

First, there is no point in misrepresentation and spin. Being less than honest with yourself or potential employers about your personality, skills or preferences might momentarily move you closer to some shiny position or other. But should you manage to bluster your way into a 'dream gig', unless that job truly matches your needs and abilities, it's not really a 'dream gig' at all. The result over time will to be to move you further away from happiness. You'll also annoy your employer and colleagues.

Second, there is no need to lie. *You are enough.* If the first truth is a warning against dishonesty, the second is a profound encouragement to job seekers. Happiness at work isn't for someone else – someone more skilled, more polished or more experienced than you. Everyone can find a fulfilling job. Just ask the 268 subjects of Vaillant's study, whose well-being correlated not at all with any traditional marker of success. All you need is (1) the desire to work hard, (2) some self-knowledge and (3) a little help in how best to present yourself to employers.

You no doubt came to this book with the first of those things. Hopefully you leave it armed with the second two. Thus equipped, your interviewer will soon know exactly *Why You*.

TEN EXTRA TECH QUESTIONS

The Internet of Things. Remote working. The rise of social media. Technology has shaken the foundations of our everyday lives. It's changed how we consume our news, how we communicate with one another, how we buy and sell things and how we entertain ourselves. And that goes for the way we work too.

In this digital age, tech skills aren't just a nice thing to have on your CV – in many industries, they're expected. And that doesn't just mean putting 'highly proficient in MS Office' in the skills section. No longer reserved for the IT department, technology has become an integral part of our everyday working lives and it's revolutionized how we work.

It's little surprise then that your interviewer might want to gauge how tech-savvy you are. Whether you're applying for a role in design or development, media or marketing, you should expect a few questions testing your technical know-how to come your way.

That's why I've included these ten additional questions in the second edition of *Why You?* – to address this growing demand for more and more of us to behave like digital natives at work.

Even if your job currently has little tech requirement, with more and more industries moving towards robotics and process automation, it can only stand you in good stead to stay ahead of the game.

And with the addition of coding to the UK curriculum back in 2014, it's only a matter of time before questions like 'Can you code?' become interview staples. For now, though, it's less about hard tech skills and more about having the right mindset. The questions in this chapter aim to find out three things:

- **How well you adapt to change and how willing you are to learn new things:** Being able to navigate the technical working environment doesn't mean you need to be a master programmer or a data whizz. The digital revolution shows no sign of relenting and that means that even the most advanced tech skills can quickly become out of date. It's much more valuable to an employer that you are open to the changes that will inevitably come.
- **Whether you know how to use the tech at your disposal in the right way:** Technology is usually created with the aim of helping us do something better or more easily. In reality, though, that's not always the case – whether it's an overflowing inbox, outdated software or information overload, it can sometimes be more of a hindrance than a help. Knowing how to use tech in the correct way to help you do your job more efficiently is a vital workplace skill in all industries.
- **How creative you are:** You might notice that a number of the questions in this section would be perfectly at home in chapter six. That's because, when it comes to harnessing the potential of new technology, being creative is an essential attribute no matter what industry you're working in.

I've said it before and I'll say it again: tech is changing the workplace – and it's creative people who lead that change.

Not all of the questions you'll find in this section focus on just one of the above traits – and that's why they fall together as a category. Effectively these questions all overlap. They will help your interviewer work out whether you've got the right mindset to hold your own in the digital workplace.

102. How do you keep up with new technology in this industry?

The Real Question: Do you keep pace with developments in technology, or do you prefer to stick to the tried and tested?

Top-line Tactic: *Don't just say, 'I use Google'. Prepare some specific examples.*

In the Information Age, things change fast. There are always new trends, tools and technologies emerging and if you don't keep your knowledge fresh, you can quickly fall behind.

Your interviewer wants to hire someone who's willing to put in the effort and stay ahead of the curve. Someone who knows about the latest developments in their industry will be better able to spot opportunities and take advantage of trends in the market, making them a more valuable employee for the business.

How you choose to respond to this question says a lot about your character, enthusiasm and ability to stay up to date with current trends. There are a number of ways you can go wrong, but the worst answer you can give is 'nothing'. Remember, the assets you're bringing to the company are your skills and knowledge. Your interviewer wants to know whether you're the kind of person who's willing to develop those skills and build on that knowledge – and bringing nothing to the table means you won't get a seat at it.

These days, there's really no excuse not to keep up. From podcasts to online courses, blogs to how-to videos, there are countless ways to stay on top of the digital game. And you can guarantee that others who are interviewing will take full advantage of all the resources on offer.

Don't be tempted to exaggerate what you do to keep current, though. It's easy to make bold claims, saying you do something that you don't, but never underestimate your interviewer's knowledge. If you do you'll risk being caught out.

It's a good idea to prepare a list of examples ahead of the interview and talk about the topics you've learnt about recently. Be specific – the more detail you can provide your potential employer with, the more credible your answer will seem. For a marketing role, that might sound something like this:

I follow all the usual industry blogs, like Hubspot and eConsultancy, but I really find that the best way to keep my skills up to date is by attending industry events. I recently went to a talk discussing how marketeers could implement virtual reality technology into their future marketing strategies. The concept of being able to place consumers in an environment where they actually experience the post-purchasing world (for example, being able to visualize furniture they're looking to buy within their home) has huge potential to drive sale conversion.

This answer sounds much more genuine and engaging than just saying you follow a few people on Twitter. It really doesn't matter how you choose to keep your skills and knowledge up to date, as long as you convince your interviewer that you put in the effort to stay up to speed.

103. What will tech do for us in the future?

The Real Question: How inventive are you? How quickly can you spot future trends?

Top-line Tactic: Show you have your eye on the horizon and you're not bogged down in the here and now.

To answer this question well, you need to show your interviewer that you know what's unfolding in the world of tech and that you're creative enough to be able to spot where new technology could really make a difference.

Some of the most successful companies to have emerged in recent years, including the likes of Netflix, Uber and AirBnB, have all revolved around disrupting traditional industries using new technology. Opportunities are opening up across all sectors, but you need to be on the ball in order to spot them and get ahead of the competition. While it's important to keep on top of the day-to-day that keeps the business ticking over, it's often new thinking that drives the biggest changes in an industry – and brings the biggest return.

Your interviewer wants to see if you're the kind of forward-thinking person who will lead change in their business. You need to show them that you're not so caught up in the every-day that you lose sight of the big picture.

That said, they don't expect you to have a crystal ball. There's no way you can know exactly what will happen in the future. When Apple released the first iPhone back in 2007, it had its fair share of critics who thought it would never take off. But even Steve Jobs couldn't have predicted the way these smartphones (now we just call them phones) would shake up the market and become the norm.

What your interviewer does want to see is whether you can think creatively and explore how emerging tech may be adopted by the company. There's much more out there than just smartphones and tablet devices – from drones to driverless cars, every year huge advances are being made in technology that are set to transform every aspect of our lives.

This is your chance to go big – your interviewer has given you a free pass to forget about the constraints of today's reality. You should already have a good idea of the latest developments in your industry. Discovering what new technology can do shouldn't be hard – a quick bit of Googling and you'll find the media is saturated with articles hypothesizing about where tech is taking us. All that's left now is to get creative – here's one example:

I'm really struck by how many charging points I see for electric cars now, so I think the growth in electric vehicles is going to have a real impact on transport and the environment. Elon Musk has made huge progress with Tesla and if he realizes his vision of producing a mass-market electric car for everyone, which may even drive itself, I think we'll see a revolution in all forms of transport.

104. Tell me about the biggest technical challenge you've come up against.

The Real Question: What kind of problems do you consider to be hard? And what is your approach to solving them?

Top-line Tactic: *Show you offer a cool head in a tough situation.*

The phrasing of this question might seem familiar by now – that's because it's a competency question that would be perfectly at home back in chapter five. As with most competency questions, this one is all about whether or not you possess the qualities needed to do the job you're interviewing for. In this case, the interviewer is specifically probing to find out whether your problem-solving skills are up to scratch.

Answering it should be pretty straightforward. All you need to do is come up with the right example and talk the interviewer through it, using the time-tested STAR technique. There should be a few examples to choose from, as we all face obstacles from time to time during our careers.

There's really no point in denying it. An answer like 'I haven't had any challenges in my career, I find everything easy,' is one of the worst you can give. Your interviewer isn't looking for someone who's so skilled they never find anything difficult, because that person simply doesn't exist. They're much more interested in finding out whether you're the type of person who's going to shy away from a challenge, or treat it as an opportunity to test yourself and learn something new.

Think carefully about which example you choose, as it will give your interviewer a lot of information about your level of experience. Much depends on the position you're applying for. For instance, if you're interviewing for a role as a developer and you're only able to provide examples of simplistic bug fixes, then you're not going to give the interviewer confidence in your ability to create elegant technical solutions. This might not be such a problem if you're interviewing for an entry-level role, but try to pick something that's appropriate to the job you're applying for.

There are lots of types of challenges you can choose from:

- A time you were presented with a challenge as part of your role.
- A time you volunteered to take on a challenge.
- A time an unexpected challenge arose and you stepped up to the plate.

It doesn't really matter which one you choose; what's important is how you explain your approach. This is where the STAR technique we learnt about at the start of the book comes in. Make sure you give your interviewer some context by explaining the Situation and the Task, talk them through your Actions and finally describe the Results. That might go something like this:

When I was working for OtherCo, during a recent website release it became apparent that our submission form had broken and we weren't receiving any responses. I was asked to urgently resolve this issue and was able to identify, debug, and release a hotfix within two hours, minimizing impact on leads and therefore revenue.

105. Tell me about a time you worked on a project involving a technology that was new to you. How did you approach it?

The Real Question: How do you overcome a lack of expertise? How easily can you adapt to change?

Top-line Tactic: *Mindset strength helps to resolve skill-set gap.*

Not all companies operate in the same way, so no matter how much experience you have, when starting a new role there's always plenty to learn. It's almost certain that there will be new processes, methods and technologies that you'll need to get to grips with.

And in any role, the unexpected can always crop up. New trends and technologies are always emerging and any skill set can quickly become out of date. You can't say what the workplace will look like in three years' time – and your interviewer doesn't know either. And that's exactly why they might ask this question.

The best way to future-proof a business is to hire people who have the right mindset to adapt to change. Someone who's willing to look outside of their skill set and learn something new will be a much more valuable employee in the long run. You need to show your interviewer that you're not afraid of treading new ground in order to tackle a gap in your knowledge, and that you know the right way to go about it to ensure you deliver.

This question fits the competency format – so it's no surprise that a great way to tackle this one is by using our old friend the STAR technique. Highlight a previous example of where you were asked to get to grips with new technology and deliver under high-pressure circumstances, and what the results were, for example:

In my last role, we onboarded a piece of marketing automation software, which enabled us to better manage new business leads. The first thing I did was to interview key stakeholders to ensure we had a clear picture of what success looked like, both in terms of commercial impact and return on investment. I then worked with an external consultant who helped us build a roll-out plan with our sales team to ensure they understood the process. Within six months our investment had more than paid for itself, the sales team really value how effectively new leads come into the business and I've become an expert in using the product.

This answer doesn't just tell the interviewer how you introduced new technology to the organization to create efficiencies. It uses a real example to plot the candidate's path from unsure and unskilled, through understanding the brief and beginning to execute, all the way to fully grasping the subject matter.

106. What's your favourite piece of software that you use to help you do your job and why?

The Real Question: How does tech allow you to work more effectively? Do you know the best software on the market to help you achieve your goals?

Top-line Tactic: *Be honest and back it up.*

The market is flooded with programs that are designed to make our jobs easier and more efficient. From Slack to Salesforce, computer software facilitates our work and saves businesses time, effort and money. Your interviewer wants to know whether you're the type of tech-savvy person who'll take advantage of technology to do their job as best they can.

This is a straight-bat question requiring a straight-bat response. Answering should be simple – be honest and select an example of a program that you've actually used before and found useful. Try to select something that's interesting and current (picking Internet Explorer might get you laughed out of the building). A good answer will take exciting new technology and make use of it in a truly efficient way. Bonus points if you know that the hiring company is currently using it.

At the moment, I can't sing the praises of Evernote enough. I like it because I can organize my to-do list and calendar in one place and it syncs with my phone and laptop, so I always know what I need to do and where I need to be and when. I recommended it to lots of people in my last role and it made sharing work with my team and line manager really straightforward.

Don't just name the newest program on the market, though – even MS Word can be a correct answer, as long as you justify it with sound reasoning, explaining why it works for you. It's also worth acknowledging any cons that are associated with the product, making it clear why they don't faze you, and mentioning alternatives to show you know what else is out there. Here's an example:

I know it sounds a bit obvious, but I really have to say my favourite piece of software is Microsoft Word. In my opinion, it's the number one word processor for a reason. I've used it every day of my working life, and all the way through university.

I know some people use Google Docs, and there's no denying that the option to store your documents online and share them with co-workers is great. However, when it comes to writing, Word, and its superior formatting functionality, works best for me.

The most important thing is that you don't lie. If your interviewer digs too deep, your lie will quickly be revealed – and even if it isn't, it could come back to bite you if you do get the job and your lack of knowledge becomes clear.

107. How do you manage remote working relationships?

The Real Question: Do you know how to use technology to benefit work relationships?

Top-line Tactic: Show your communication skills span beyond the office floor.

Whether you're telecommuting from your sofa or tweeting from the Alps, remote working requires extra effort to keep up communication. When there's no option to drop by someone's desk for a quick chat, or catch up on the latest project between meetings, connecting and collaborating online is absolutely vital. And even if you're on site, there's a high probability that you'll have to work with those who aren't – whether that's far-away colleagues, international teams or external agencies.

The good news is that the technology to facilitate remote working has come on leaps and bounds in the past decade. Gone are the days of waiting for webcams to buffer and faxes to be sent through. In the modern workplace, online chat, email, video hangouts and project management software are all an integral part of the day-to-day, and knowing how to use them in the most effective way is a valuable skill.

Your interviewer is asking this question to gauge whether you're familiar with any of the tools on offer and how proficient you are in using them. Your answer should aim to convince them that you're a pro-active communicator who knows what tools to use and when. A good answer will reference a range of relevant communication platforms and when they should be used:

If I have a quick question I need to ask another member of the team, I'll usually drop them a message on chat. But if it's something I'll need to refer back to later – like deadlines, meeting dates or agreements in writing – then I'll use email. If there's something that the whole team is collaborating on, I find project management software, like Asana, is a great way to manage a group project remotely. And for face-to-face meetings with colleagues off site – whether it's an interview, brainstorming a project or an informal chat – video hangouts are a fantastic tool. Sometimes things can get lost in typed communication, so in certain situations it's much easier to interpret the tone of a conversation if you're speaking directly.

This answer ticks a number of boxes. First of all, it shows your interviewer that you're familiar with a number of different technologies and you take advantage of what's out there. Second, it shows that you know how to use these tools in different ways that are appropriate to different situations. Using video chat when you need written confirmation from the other person? Maybe not the best idea. And finally, it shows that you consider the needs of others and know what works best when it comes to collaborating.

108. How would you improve our website/app?

The Real Question: Have you done your research? And what added value and insight will you bring to the business?

Top-line Tactic: *Give constructive feedback not flattery.*

This question is essentially the techy twin to *What will your skills and ideas bring to the company?* Its purpose is to help your interviewer figure out whether you have ideas they could benefit from, and if you can add value to the organization. Once again, the right approach is to be open and bring your A-game to the table. Don't be afraid of revealing your best ideas – without them, you'll risk your chance of landing the job.

This is your chance to demonstrate how you'd change the company for the better, so make sure you're prepared ahead of time and come armed with plenty of ideas. These days, most brands and businesses have a digital presence, whether it's a website or an app, a YouTube channel or an Instagram page, so there's no excuse not to check them out before you turn up for the interview.

Consider what you think the company does well and, most importantly, where there's room for improvement. This isn't the moment for flattery – your interviewer doesn't want to hear that you love the website and wouldn't change a thing. Playing teacher's pet will only put you at risk of coming across as void of innovative ideas, not to mention seeming overeager.

However, it goes without saying that you should err on the side of caution when it comes to tearing the current business offering apart. You're here to get hired, not to make the interviewer question why you'd want the job in the first place.

Instead, look to small, quick wins that you could help the company make in your first few months on the job. Don't just identify problems that you see, though; you need to offer solutions and ideas for improvement as well. By doing so, you'll help the interviewer to start visualizing you making a real impact in their business.

If possible, you should try to tie your answer back to something you've done in a previous role. Incorporating examples of things you've done before shows your interviewer that you can deliver on your ideas – much more desirable in an employee than someone who's all talk and no action.

When I was browsing your website, I noticed that there's no inter-linking between the cookery book and kitchen utensil product pages. In my previous position at RetailInc we had a similar issue arise where the hiking and waterproof sections shared no digital relationship. I recommended cross-merchandizing them to see if average purchase order value increased – which it did by 25 per cent. As there are items in both of your kitchen-related categories that complement one another, I think it would be a good idea to implement the same approach.

Even if something seems obvious to you, a fresh pair of eyes can turn up issues that are hiding in plain sight for an established team, so don't hold back. Perhaps you've seen some cumbersome code on the website, or noticed the styling is out of sync when using the app? Wherever you can add value, do so here.

109. If you were a tech brand, which one would you be and why?

The Real Question: Who do you think you are? What are your values?

Top-line Tactic: *Match your brand values to the hiring company and the role you're interviewing for.*

In the first instance, this question might throw you off. And it's no surprise. This one's a curious combo – part curveball, part character-based question – that interviewers use to catch you off guard and get you to reveal your true self. Less straightforward than asking you outright about what your values are, it has an added layer of complexity that gets you thinking on your feet.

Like most curveballs, the focus here is more on how you reason out your answer and less on the answer you actually give. Nonetheless, there are a few ways you can go wrong when selecting which brand you identify with. Try to avoid choosing anything outdated or obsolete, or you'll risk seeming out of touch with current market trends. And it's best to stay away from any brands with controversial or dubious connotations, such as alcohol or cigarettes – it may seem funny at the time, but you might regret the association.

Industry-leading brands are usually preferable, as your interviewer is more likely to understand an association with a brand they already have an awareness of. If you must choose a more obscure brand that's a personal favourite, then make sure you explain to your interviewer exactly what the brand does within its niche market that you like.

The most important thing is that you back up your answer with some well-thought-out character traits that link back to the brand. To really impress, you should highlight personal traits that align to the values of the company and make sure they're relevant for the role you're interviewing for. That means you'll need to know what the company stands for and understand the job you're applying for. It's vital that you do your research and read the job description thoroughly before the interview.

For a marketing role at a tech-focused company, that might sound something like this:

I would be Twitter, because I'm always in touch with whatever's trending, I'm an enthusiastic communicator who can make a point succinctly and I make connections with all sorts of people.

For a UX designer, that might sound something like this:

I would be Amazon, because I put customer experience at the centre of everything I do, I always deliver on time and I'm an early adopter – oh, and I'm prepared to swallow the odd unfavourable review.

Curveballs like these are a great way for interviewers to gauge a candidate's sense of humour, so don't be afraid to be funny – it'll make you memorable. This is your chance to really sell your personality, stand out from the competition and show why you're a good fit for the hiring company, so don't waste it.

110. If you could create an app that could do anything to improve your life, what would it be?

The Real Question: How creative are you? How easily can you relate technology to an everyday problem?

Top-line Tactic: *Demonstrate your ability to single out and satisfy a unique consumer need.*

By now you should be familiar with this kind of question that overlaps between the curveball and creativity categories – we've already tackled a number of them in chapter six. As with all such questions, this one's being used to put you under pressure and assess your creativity and problem-solving skills.

This one has another dimension, because it's also evaluating your ability to relate a technological solution to an everyday pain point or problem. Your interviewer isn't expecting you to come up with a bestselling app on the spot – if you could do that, then your interviewer might be wondering why you haven't already made it. They just want to see if you're creative enough to come up with an answer to an everyday headache.

Try not to pick a problem that will make you look bad – if you say you need an app to find your possessions because you're always losing things, you could come across as disorganized. Otherwise, it doesn't really matter what you choose to improve. Just make sure you demonstrate a creative approach to using app technology to fix it. Here are a couple of examples:

My son has a food allergy, so I'd love to create an app which lets me scan barcodes when I'm in the supermarket so I'd know instantly if I should avoid a product.

I recently moved to a new home with a small, but very overgrown, garden. I'm in the process of tidying it up but I don't know anything about plants, so I'd love to create an app which lets me photograph a leaf or a flower and instantly tells me if it's a weed or not.

111. How would you explain a database to an eight-year-old in three sentences?

The Real Question: How easily can you break down complicated concepts? How good are your communication skills?

Top-line Tactic: *Forget the jargon and take things back to basics.*

This is another curveball cooked up by Google, which they've previously used to test interviewees. However, that doesn't mean you won't find it being wheeled out by interviewers elsewhere, so it's good to be prepared. Depending on the role you're applying for it can crop up under a number of guises, so you can replace 'database' with any technical term that's relevant to your industry.

Unlike some of Google's other brainteasers, this curveball question tells the interviewer more about you than just how creative you are under pressure (although it does that too). Being able to convey complex concepts in simple terms is a valuable skill, particularly in this jargon-filled age.

One of the best and worst things to come out of the growth of technology is the emergence of a whole new digital lexicon – to an outsider it can seem like another language. If you thought getting to grips with the term 'selfie' was novel, then understanding the meaning of 'search engine optimization' is a whole other ballgame. And don't get me started on SQL syntax . . .

It all comes down to clear communication. When you're working with lots of different teams who all have their own jargon, being able to communicate clearly with one another is key to allowing you to go about your job more efficiently.

And clear communication isn't just important in the office; it's also a really useful skill when it comes to speaking to your audience. A lot of tech companies rely on complex technologies that they market to a mass audience, so being able to turn complicated ideas into something that's easily used and understood is vital. It pays to be able to simplify.

In your answer, you need to use easy-to-understand logic and facts. Your interviewer already knows what a database is – they're not testing you on the information itself, they're testing you on your ability to summarize it. The key is knowing what is (and what isn't) valuable information. Here's one example:

A database is a lot like the toy chest where you keep your toys – except that the toys are data instead.

When you've finished playing with your toys, you put them all away neatly in the toy chest so you can find them easily the next time you want to play with them.

In this way, the toy chest is your database, grouping all the different types of toys in a sensible order – whether that's all the car toys or all the cuddly bears – so you can quickly find them again.

It's hard to come up with something this clever on the spot, so don't be afraid to pause for thought before you answer. You've only got three sentences, so use them wisely.

ACKNOWLEDGEMENTS

I would especially like to thank Grace Donnelly, Jason Dunne, Joseph Hughes, Tiffany Koyas and Jessica Stillman for doing the 'heavy lifting' for this book; I could not have completed it without you. I would also like to thank my agent, Jill Marsal, and the team at Penguin, in particular Joel Rickett, Richard Lennon and Trevor Horwood, for their excellent advice and editorial input. The research that was conducted to create the text was crowdsourced, as I described in Chapter 1, and it would not have been written without the help and contribution of everyone listed below. Thank you.

Chris Addison, Waqas Ahmad, Latoya Akerele, Tobi Akintokun, Chris Alexander, Olivia Alexander, Ash Ali, Helen Argent, Peter Arkell, Mel Armstrong, Kamaljit Arora, Deborah Ashmore, Phil Ashwell, Kishor Athale, Jamie Atkins, John Ayton, Elanor Baddeley, Simon Baddeley, Louisa Baker, Anita Bangar, Christina Baptista, Cathy Barlow, Laura Barnes, Laura Barrat, Paul Barter, Caroline Batchelor, Chris Batten, Gavin Beart, Rehena Begum, Amanda Benbelaid, Marie Bennell, Ross Bennie, Kuldeep Bhandal, Vickie Birnage, Simon Black, Christopher Blackburn, Brigid Blair, Agnieszka Bohdanowicz, Jade Bouch, Alexandra Bowen, Will Bowley, Joanne Boyd-White, Anita Boyle, Gary Bradley, Claire Brand, Nicola

Brand, Neville Brauer, Terence Brazier, Sian Breward, Barbara Breytenbach, Tracy Britten, John Brooks, Debbie Brown, Iain Brown, Jojo Brown, Jonathan Brown, Lisa Brown, Debbie Browne, Conrad Brunton, Lisa Bryan, Denise Buchan, Nigel Buck, Mark Buckle, Jaap Buitendijk, Tristan Bullworthy, Tom Bunkham, Gavan Burden, Kate Burgess, Aura Burghiu, Martin Burkitt, Rebecca Burling, Jane Burrows, Louise Buson, Lynn Cahillane, Nikki Cameron, Adam Campbell, Callum Carscadden, Lucy Carter, Susan Carthew, Katie Cartner, Mike Cheary, Rebecca Clacy-Jones, Donna Clapton, Jon Clark, Phil Clarke, Sarah Clarke, Keith Cleverley, Emma Coates, Jose Cofone, Megan Cohen, Sonia Coleman, Peter Collins, Jennifer Collis, Richard Connolly, Hannah Cooper, Jack Cooper, Sarah Cooper, Lee Costello, Tim Court, Amy Cowley, Nicki Cresdee, Krisztina Csanaky, Jose Cupertino, Ashley Curzon, Paresh Dabasia, John Darby, Dario Dasilva, Chris Davies, Matthew Davies, Ray Dawes, Dan Dawson, Kelly De Vroede-Strong, Tracey Deakin, Gary Dean-Andrews, Pat Deeley, Lewis Dee-Thomas, Maria Delgado, Heidi Dennis, Olga Dennis, Sarah Dennis, Ros Denton, Jed Dillon, Tatiana Dimopoulou, Adam Diprose, Amy Dodsworth, Ryan Doel, Peter Donaldson, Clare Donovan, Neil Dorset, Boris Drappier, Monika Drevenakova, Hayley Duckworth, Tom Dudman, Mark Duffey, Ashley Dukes, Steve Dungworth, Suzanne Dunne, Maria Dyer, James Eastwood, Kris Eastwood, Bradley Ebsworth-Willis, Natalie Edgell, Derek Eelloo, Evelyn Eichmuller, Richard Elliott, Daniel Ellis, Eve Ellison, Ned Ellison, Yasmina Ely, Laura Errington, Carly Evans, Kayleigh Eve, Mariam Ezzat, Lee Fallon, Martin Fallon, Yusef Fanous, Gabor Farkas, Iram Farooq, Abdulsaheed Fatungase, Andy Ferguson, Abbey Fielder, Lewis Finch, Victoria Finnegan, Lesley Finnih, Ralph Finnon, Jamie Fish, Nikki Fisher, Tracy Fisher, Dorine Flies, Helen Fontaine, Jo Foord, Amy Foster, Katrina Fox, Duncan Frankham, Sian

ACKNOWLEDGEMENTS

Franklin, Vlad Fratila, Ben Fuller, Frances Galbraith, Bosco Garcia-Valenzuela, Holly Gardner, Sharon Gay, Peter Geary, Nguepkep Wandji Ghislaine, David Gilroy, Nadine Gittens, Biagio Gizzi, Amy Glastonbury-Cole, Komlan Gnamatsi, Jody Goble, Bradley Gold, Nick Goodman, Yulisa Gordon, Sue Gouldman, Joe Graham, Neil Graham, Victor Granville, Michelle Green, Oliver Green, Douglas Greer, Rochelle Gregory, Vicky Grovenor, Lauren Guy, Peter Gyoury, Sally Hall, Will Hall, Mandi Halton, Rik Hamilton, Ben Hanley, Neil Hardy, John Harold, Neil Harris, Paul Harvey, Pamela Hassall, Louise Hatcher, Matt Heather, Jeff Henderson, Jon Herbert, Nicola Hewitt, Katherine Highton, Timo Hilhorst, Adam Hill, David Hill, Lisa Himsworth, Peter Hinkson, Linda Hitchcock, Jim Hoare, Dave Holby-Wolinski, James Holt, Lisa Hooper, Jill Houghton, Collette Huckle, Daryl Hughes, Tom Hughes, Josh Hunt, Charlotte Hutchings, Dominic Hyde, Colin Ingleton, Ray Iqbal, Julie Jack, Louise Jackson, Nesh Jain, Lisa James, Charlotte Jarman, Dan Jenkins, David Jobe, Lee Johnson, John Jones, Michael Jones, Naz Junaid, Muhammad Kashif, Katie Kay, Martin Kendall, Paul Kenna, George Kenny, Michelle Kenton, Tina Kessie, Tim King, Lucinda Kooi, Zuzana Kosorinova, Mike Kufluk-Thackery, Ravindra Kumar, Terri Lalonde, Bev Lambert, Christine Lambert, Tim Lane, Kim Lansdell, Agnes LaPlume, Chang Lau, Ken Lau, Marilyn Laurence, Soraya Lavery, Laarni Agustin Laxamana, Kerren Leach, Andy Lee, Daniel Lee, Harry Lee, Karen Lee, Chris Legge, Jeremy Lennard, Catherine Lennie, Charlton Leung, Ariel Lewis, Michelle Lewis, Stuart Lindenfield, Stuart Lindsay, Steven Linpow, Harry Liosis, Candida Lobato, Jean Lofulo, Tom Lovell, Jonathan Low-Hang, James Luff, Richard Luffman, Justin Lush, Kirsty Macgregor, Jenni Mackenzie, Scott Macrae, John Maguire, David Mains, Judy Mallinson, Tilly Marchington, Mary Marcus, Kirsty Marsh, Richard Marsh,

ACKNOWLEDGEMENTS

Alina Martsak, Catherine Maskell, Yvonne May, Paul Maynard, Mandy Mbelu, Stephen McCarty, Lou McCaul, Maria McElvenney, Alastair McFarlane, Daniel McLean, Danielle McNulty, John McNulty, Jon Meeks, Sarah Megarity, Afrecia Meikle, Josh Menham, Madeleine Menzies, Sophie Mercer, Tom Millar, Jonathan Mills, Ian Molloy, Natasha Monaghan, Tania Monks, Amy Moore, Kieran Moore, William Moore, Jenny Morgan, Georgina Morley, Sarah Mortimer, Norma Mulligan, Adam Munro, Lee Murphy, Meg Murphy, Donna Murrell, Sera Myung, Joe Neilson, Barbara Nesbitt, Jaret Nicholls, Shane Nicholson, Tracey Noblett, Gail Norman, Amy Norris, Dee Nsubuga, Anna O'Neill, Russ Oliver, Damien Ollerhead, Chimezie Onyirioha, Alex Osborne, Anna Otubambo, Valentina Pangratiou, Tiffany Parradine, Cristina Pastor, Horus Patel, Lisa Patient, Daniel Paul, Natalie Paul, Paul Pegler, Liz Penemo, Leigh Penfold, Rui Pereira, Phillipa Perry, Jo Pertwee, Max Peters, Sophie Peterson, Leigh Phillips, Anish Pillai, Joanne Pink, Bill Porter, Richard Post, Adrian Potkins, Emma Potts, Dave Poulter, Chris Powell, Wendy Prangnell, Justin Preston, Andrew Price, Sam Proctor, Richard Pucci, Oliver Queisser, Stuart Quinn, Dominic Quirke, Jon Rabbett, Shuborna Rahman, Angela Raja-Ross, Rina Rathod, Matt Ratledge, Vitaliya Raubaite, Ben Read, Abi Reed, Nicola Reed, Tabitha Reed, Debbie Reeves, Emma Reid, Lizzy Reid, Mark Rhodes, Tristan M. Rich, Sonia Richards, Zoe Richards, James Richardson, Matthew Richardson, Myra Rickard, Mark Ridley, David Roach, Sandy Roach, Christopher Roberts, Emma Roberts, Karl Roberts, Megan Roberts, Helen Robertson, David Robinson, Drew Robinson, Ed Robinson, Ella Robinson, Helen Robinson, Ray Robinson, Sophie Robinson, Amber Rolfe, Julie Rose, Michael Round, Matthew Rowe, John Rowlands, Jez Rule, Krishna Ruparelia, Matt Rushton, Melissa Russ, Andrew Russell, Simon Ryan, Aimee Ryder, Matt Ryder, Matthew Sagar,

ACKNOWLEDGEMENTS

Rav Sall, Katrina Salter, David E. Salva, Amar Sandhu, Jeff Scott, Paul Scott, Rory Scott, Navaz Sethna, Luke Sewell, Manal Shamallakh, Tyler Shane, Suraj Sharma, Matt Sharman, Ruth Shaw, John Shenton, Chloe Sheppard, Russell Singh, Harpal Sira, David Slatter, Ursula Sloan, Jason Smith, Martin Smith, Richard Smith, George Sofokleous, Rakhee Soni, Phil Southern, Melinda Spencer, Mihaela Spirova, Con Stack, Cath Stanway, Lucy Stephens, Carly Stewart, Howard Stiles, Sarah Stimson, Rachael Stones, Lydia Stott, Kate Stratful, Emma Strong, Mark Stuart, Beau Sukpran, Joe Sweeney, Nick Tagg, Paul Talbot, Chloe Taylor, Janet Taylor, Michelle Taylor, Nancy Taylor, David Thatcher, Marie-Clara Thaureux, Dunstan Thomas, Esme Thomas, James Thomas, Miles Thresher, Daniel Tindal, Suzie Tobias, David Todd, Linda Tomlinson, Gilly Trevena, David Trewin, Ashley Trunley, Kirsty Turnbull, Chris Turner, Martin Turner, Ruth Turner, Marcus Tutin, Bharti Vadher, Tasha Valenzuela, Rachael Varney, Nicola Vaughan, Christos Vayonitis, Marianela Vermeer, Amanda Vickers, Ruth Victorin, Rupal Vyas, Lee-Ann Waddington, Raju Wahid, Laura Wainwright, Hayley Walker, Sue Walker, Jessica Walsh, Steve Walters, Jenny Walton, Victoria Ward, Esther Ware, Martin Warnes, Chris Warren, Diane Warren, Dona Warren, Glenn Watts, Leslie Weare, Krystina Webb, Sarah Webb, Duncan Welch, Andrew Welsh, Dean Whittington, Huw Williams, Peter Williams, Stephen Wilshaw, Karen Wilson, Simon Wilson, John Window, Nannette Windsor, Adam Woodbridge, Gladys Wright, Tracy Wright, Greg Wyatt, Paul Young.

If you have been interviewed recently, please email me at james@jamesreed.com or tweet using #WhyYou and tell me which questions you were asked – your help will be greatly appreciated and will make future editions even more definitive.

James Reed & Dr Paul Stoltz

PUT YOUR MINDSET TO WORK: The One Asset You Really Need to Win and Keep the Job You Love

What's the real secret of successful job hunters?

In these unstable times, everyone wants to stand out from the crowd and secure a rewarding job with long-term potential. But what does it actually take to get the job you want? Ninety-seven percent of employers argue that it goes beyond having the right skills - it's all about the right *mindset*.

James Reed, chairman of recruitment giant Reed, knows what employers really want from the people they hire and promote. With bestselling author Paul Stoltz, he has now identified exactly what makes you more likely to succeed when you're job hunting.

In this book, Reed and Stoltz explain the '3G Mindset' - the way to develop the traits that will set you apart from the herd. Their powerful tools will help you assess your own mindset, and show employers your *true* value.

'If you want to work for the best, mindset is *everything*' Stephen Burrill, Deloitte

'The insights in this brilliant book could have saved me and any top employer a lot of elementary mistakes, never mind the additional cost of bad decisions' Gordon Roddick, Co-Founder, The Body Shop

'This brilliant book equips anyone wanting a leg up at work and in life with the tools to flourish. Mindset beats skillset every time' John Ainley, Aviva

'This book is a game changer. Read it, remember it, and put your new 3G Mindset to work. There'll be no stopping you' James Timpson, Managing Director, Timpsons

'People who thrive at Facebook have to have the right mindset, period. That's what's driving us into the future. This book shows you how to gauge it and get it' Caitlin Dooley, Facebook

---